THE PRACTICE OF JUSTICE OUR ONLY SECURITY FOR THE FUTURE.

REMARKS

OF

ON. WILLIAM D. KELLEY,

OF PENNSYLVANIA,

IN SUPPORT OF HIS PROPOSED AMENDMENT

TO THE BILL

GUARANTY TO CERTAIN STATES WHOSE GOVERNMENTS HAVE BEEN USURPED OR OVERTHROWN A REPUBLICAN FORM OF GOVERNMENT;"

DELIVERED

IN THE HOUSE OF REPRESENTATIVES, JANUARY 16, 1865.

WASHINGTON:
1865.

REMARKS.

The House having under consideration the bill "to guaranty to certain States whose governments have been usurped or overthrown a republican form of government," Mr. Kelley moved to amend the bill by inserting after the words "to enroll all the white male citizens of the United States" the words "and all other male citizens of the United States who may be able to read the constitution thereof," and said:

Mr. Speaker, These are indeed terrible times for timid people. Use and wont no longer serve us. The guns traitorously fired upon Fort Sumter threw us all out of the well-beaten ruts of habit, and as the war progresses men find themselves less and less able to express their political views by naming a party or uttering its shibboleth. It is no longer safe for any of us to wait till the election comes and accept the platform and tickets presented by a party. We may have served in its ranks for a life-time and find at last—costly and painful experience being our guide—that to obtain the ends we had in view we should have acted independently of, and in opposition to it and its leaders. In seasons like this, an age on ages telling, the feeblest man in whom there is faith or honesty is made to feel that he is not quite powerless, that duty is laid on him too, and that the force that is in him ought to be expressed in accordance with his own convictions and in a way to promote some end seen or hoped for.

The questions with which we have to deal, the grave doubts that confound us, the difficulties that environ us, the results our action will produce, fraught with weal or woe to centuries and constantly-increasing millions, are such as have rarely been confided to a generation. But happily we are not without guidance. Our situation, though novel, does not necessarily cast us upon the field of mere experiment. True, we have not specific precedents which we may safely follow; but the founders of our Government gave us, in a few brief sentences, laws by which we may extricate our generation and country from the horrors that involve them, and secure peace broad as our country, enduring as its history, and beneficent as right and justice and love.

The organized war power of the rebellion is on the eve of overthrow. It belongs to us to govern the territory we have conquered, and the question of reconstruction presses itself upon our attention; and our legislation in this behalf will, though it comprise no specific provisions on the subject, determine whether guerrilla war shall harass communities for long years, or be suppressed in a brief time by punishments administered through courts and law, to marauders for the crimes they may commit under the name of partisan warfare. At the close of an international war, the wronged but victorious party may justly make two claims: indemnity for the past, and security for the future; indemnity for the past in money or in territory; security for the future by new treaties, the establishment of new boundaries, or the cession of military power and the territory upon which it dwells. Indemnity for the past we cannot hope to obtain. When we shall have punished the conspirators who involved the country in this sanguinary war, and pardoned the dupes and victims who have arrayed themselves or been forced to do battle under their flag, we shall but have repossessed our ancient territory, reëstablished the boundaries of our country, restored to our flag and Constitution their supremacy over territory which was ours, but which the insurgents meant to dismember and possess. The other demand we may and must successfully make. Security for the future is accessible to us, and we must demand it; and to obtain it with amplest guarantees requires the adoption of no new idea, the making of no experiment, the entering upon no sea of political speculation. Ours would have been an era of peace and prosperity, had we and our fathers accepted in full faith the great principles that impelled their fathers to demand the independence of the United Colonies, gave them strength in counsel, patience, courage, and long endurance in the field, and guided them in establishing a Constitution which all ages will recognize as the miracle of the era in which it was framed and adopted, and the influence of which shall modify and change, and bring into its own similitude, the Governments of the world. Had we, and the generation that preceded us, accepted and been guided by the self-evident truths to which I allude, the world would never have known the martial power of the American people, or realized the fact that a Government that sits so lightly as ours upon the people in peace is so infinitely strong in the terrible season of war.

The founders of our institutions labored consciously and reverently in the sight of God. They knew that they were the creatures of His power, and that their work could only be well done by being done in the recognition of His attributes, and in harmony with the enduring laws of His providence. They knew that His ways were ways of pleasantness, and His paths the paths of peace; and they endeavored to embody His righteousness and justice in the Government they were fashioning for unknown ages, and untold millions of men. Their children, in the enjoyment of the prosperity thus secured to them, lost their faith in these great truths, treated them with utter disregard, violated them, legislated in opposition to them, and finally strove to govern the country in active hostility to them. And for a little while they seemed to succeed. But at length we have been made to feel and know that God's justice does not sleep always; and amid the ruins of the country and the desolation of our homes let us resolve that we will return to the ancient ways, look to Him for guidance, and follow humbly in the footsteps of our wise and pious forefathers; and that, as grateful children, we will erect to their memory and to that of the brave men who have died in defense of their work in this the grandest of all wars, a monument broad as our country, pure as was their wisdom, and enduring as Christian civilization. So shall we by our firmness and equity exalt the humble, restrain the rapacious and arrogant, and bind the people to each other by the manifold cords of common sympathies and interest, and to the Government by the gratitude due to a just and generous guardian.

But, Mr. Speaker, I hear gentlemen inquire how this is to be done. The process is simple, easy, and inviting: it is by accepting in child-like faith, and executing with firm and steady purpose three or four of the simple dogmas which the founders of our Government proclaimed to the world, and which, alas! too often with hypocritical lip service, are professed by all Americans, even those who are now striving, through blood, and carnage, and devastation, to found a broad empire, the corner-stone of which was to be human slavery.

In announcing the reasons which impelled the colonies to a separation from the mother country, the American people declared that "a decent respect to the opinions of mankind" required "a declaration of the causes which impelled them to the separation;" and in assigning those causes announced a few general propositions, embodying eternal and ever-operating principles, among which were,

First, that "all men are created equal, are endowed with certain inalienable rights," and that "among these are life, liberty, and the pursuit of happiness;"

Second, that "to insure these rights, Governments are instituted among men;"

Third, that "Governments derive their just powers from the consent of the governed;"

Fourth, that "whenever any form of government becomes destructive of these ends, it is the right of the people to alter or to abolish it, and to institute a new Government, laying its foundations on such principles and organizing its powers in such form as to them shall seem most likely to effect their safety and happiness." And in these four propositions we have an all-sufficient guide to enduring peace and prosperity. If in the legislation we propose we regard these self-evident truths, our posterity shall not only enjoy peace, but teach the world the way to universal freedom; but if we fail to regard them, God alone in His infinite wisdom knows what years of agitation, war, and misery we may entail on posterity, and whether the overthrow of our Government, the division of our country, and all the ills thus entailed on mankind may not be justly chargeable to us.

The tables of the census of 1860 exhibiting the population of the eleven insurgent States, show that it numbered, and was divided as follows:

States.	White population.	Colored population, slave and free, including Indians.
Alabama	526,271	436,930
Arkansas	324,143	111,307
Florida	77,74[illegible]	62,677
Georgia	591,550	465,736
Louisiana	357,456	350,546
Mississippi	353,901	437,404
North Carolina	629,942	362,680
South Carolina	291,300	412,408
Tennessee	826,722	283,079
Texas	420,891	183,324
Virginia	1,047,299	549,019
	5,447,222	3,666,110

This table, as will be observed, embraces the whole of Virginia as she was in 1860; and as I have not the means of distinguishing the proportion of her population that is embraced in the new State of West Virginia, I permit it to stand as it is. The new State is in the Union; her citizens never assented to the ordinance of secession; they have provided for the extinguishment of slavery within her limits; and my remarks, save in the general scope in which they may be applicable to any or all of the States of the Union, will not be understood as applying to her. It is of the territory for which it is the duty of Congress to provide governments that I speak. I should also call attention to the fact that the Superintendent of the Census includes the few Indians that remained in some of these States in the column of white inhabitants. Their number is not important; but it certainly should not be so stated as to create the impression that they enjoyed the rights or performed the duties of citizens. How unfair this classification is will appear from the fact that the following section from the Code of Tennessee of 1858, section 3,858, indicates very fairly the position they held under the legislation of each and all the above-named States:

"A negro, mulatto, *Indian*, or person of mixed blood,

descended from negro or Indian ancestors, to the third generation inclusive, though one ancestor of each generation may have been a white person, whether bond or free, is incapable of being a witness in any case, civil or criminal, except for or against each other."

Correcting the error of the Superintendent of the Census, I have enumerated the Indians with the people to whose fate the legislation of those States assigned them. It will be perceived that when that census was taken the white population numbered 5,447,222, and the colored population 3,666,110.

It thus appears that the colored people were considerably more than two fifths of the whole population of the insurgent States; and that while we have professed to believe that their right to life, liberty, and the pursuit of happiness was inalienable—could not be alienated or relinquished by them, nor taken away by others—we have ignored their humanity, and denied them the enjoyment of any single political right.

That, while we have professed to believe that governments are instituted among men to secure their rights, the history of our country for the last fifty years proves that the whole power and constant labor of our Government have been exerted to prevent the possibility of two fifths of the people of more than half our country ever attaining the enjoyment of political, civil, or social rights.

That, while we have professed to believe that all Governments derive their just powers from the consent of the governed, we have punished with ignominy and stripes and imprisonment and death the men who had the temerity to assert that it was wrong to deny to two fifths of the people of a country, and, as in the case of South Carolina and Mississippi, a large majority of the people of the State, the right even to petition for redress of grievance.

And while we have been swift to assure, in terms of warmest sympathy, and sometimes with active aid, any oppressed and revolting people beyond the seas that we believed it to be the right and duty of such people, "whenever any form of Government becomes destructive of the ends" above indicated, "to alter or abolish it, and to institute a new Government, laying its foundations on such principles, and organizing its powers in such form, as to them shall seem most likely to effect their safety and happiness," we have, even to the boundaries of the lakes and to the far Pacific shores, stood pledged and ready to lay down our lives in the suppression of any attempt these Americans might make to carry into effect this cardinal doctrine of our professed political faith. Is it any wonder that God, seeing millions of His people thus trampled on, oppressed, outraged, and made voiceless by those whose fathers had placed their feet in His ways, and whose lips never wearied in beseeching His guidance and care, should fill the oppressors with madness and open through their blood and agony a way for the deliverance of their long-suffering victims?

But, Mr. Speaker, it is asked, who are these people? They are the laboring masses of the South—the field hand, the house servant, the mechanic, the artisan, the engineer of that region. Their sinewy arms have felled the forest, opened the farm and the plantation, made the road, the canal, the railroad. It was by the sweat of their brow that the sunny South was made to bloom; it is they whose labor has quickened the wheels of commerce and swelled the accumulating wealth of the world. Upon their brawny shoulders rested the social fabric of the South, and an arrogant aristocracy, that strove to dictate morals to the world, boasted that one product of their toil was a king to whom peoples and Governments must bow. Most of them are ignorant and degraded; but that cannot be mentioned to their disgrace or disparagement. Not they nor their ancestors enacted the laws which made it a felony to enable them to read the Constitution and the laws of their country, or the Book of Life through which their fairer brethren hope for salvation. Dumb and voiceless most of them are; but let not want of intellectual power be ascribed to them as a race, in view of the wit, humor, sarcasm, and pathos, of the learning, logical power, and scientific attainments, of a Douglass, a Garnet, a Remond, a Brown, a Sella Martin, a William Craft, and scores of others, who, evading the bloodhound and his master in the slave-hunt, have made their way to lands where the teachings of Christ are regarded and the brotherhood of man is not wholly denied. Others of them are and have been free, at least so far as to be able to acquire property and send their children to foreign lands for culture. Let some such speak for themselves. In the petition of the colored citizens of Louisiana to the President and Congress of the United States, they respectfully submit:

"That they are natives of Louisiana and citizens of the United States; that they are loyal citizens, sincerely attached to the country and the Constitution, and ardently desire the maintenance of the national unity, for which they are ready to sacrifice their fortunes and their lives.

"That a large portion of them are owners of real estate, and all of them are owners of personal property; that many of them are engaged in the pursuits of commerce and industry, while others are employed as artisans in various trades; that they are all fitted to enjoy the privileges and immunities belonging to the condition of citizens of the United States, and among them may be found many of the descendants of those men whom the illustrious Jackson styled his 'fellow-citizens' when he called upon them to take up arms to repel the enemies of the country.

"Your petitioners further respectfully represent that over and above the right which, in the language of the Declaration of Independence, they possess to liberty and the pursuit of happiness, they are supported by the opinion of just and loyal men, especially by that of Hon. Edward Bates, Attorney General, in the claim to the right of enjoying the privileges and immunities pertaining to the condition of citizens of the United States; and, to support the legitimacy of this claim, they believe it simply necessary to submit to your Excellency, and to the honorable Congress, the following considerations, which they beg of you to weigh in the balance of law and justice. Notwithstanding their forefathers served in the Army of the United States, in 1814–15, and aided in repelling from the soil of Louisiana a haughty enemy, over-confident of success, yet they and their descendants have ever since, and until the era of the present rebellion, been estranged and even repulsed, excluded from all franchises, even the smallest, when their brave forefathers offered their bosoms to the enemy to preserve the territorial integrity of the Republic! During this period of forty-nine years they have never ceased to be peaceable citizens, paying their taxes on an assessment of more than fifteen million dollars!

"At the call of General Butler they hastened to rally under the banner of the Union and liberty; they have spilled their blood, and are still pouring it out for the maintenance of the Constitution of the United States; in a word, they are soldiers of the Union, and they will defend it so long as their hands have strength to hold a musket.

"While General Banks was at the siege of Port Hudson and the city threatened by the enemy, his Excellency Governor Shepley called for troops for the defense of the city, and they were foremost in responding to the call, having raised the first regiment in the short space of forty-eight hours.

"In consideration of this fact, as true and as clear as the sun which lights this great continent, in consideration of the services already performed and still to be rendered by them to their common country, they humbly beseech your Excellency and Congress to cast your eyes upon a loyal population, awaiting with confidence and dignity the proclamation of those inalienable rights which belong to the condition of citizens of the great American Republic.

"Theirs is but a feeble voice claiming attention in the midst of the grave questions raised by this terrible conflict; yet, confident of the justice which guides the action of the Government, they have no hesitation in speaking what is prompted by their hearts: 'We are men; treat us as such.'"

This petition, which it is within my knowledge was prepared by one of the proscribed race, asks only for what the fathers of our country intended they should enjoy. They discovered in the Africo-American the attributes and infirmities of their own nature, and in organizing governments, local or general, made no invidious distinction between him and his fellow-men. Under the Articles of Confederation, and at the time of the adoption of the Constitution of the United States, and long subsequent thereto, the free colored man was with their consent a citizen and a voter. Our fathers meant that he should be so. Their faith in the great cardinal maxims they enunciated was undoubting; and they embodied it without mental reservation when they gave form and action to our Government. No one who has studied the history of that period doubts that they regarded slavery as transitory and evanescent. Neither the word "slave," nor any synonym for it, was given place in the Constitution. We know by the oft-quoted remark of Mr. Madison that it was purposely excluded that the future people of the country might never be reminded by that instrument that so odious a condition had ever existed among the people of the United States. That instrument nowhere contemplates any discrimination in reference to political or personal rights on the ground of color. In defining the rights guarantied by the Constitution they are never limited to the white population, but the word "people" is used without qualification. When in that instrument its framers alluded to those who filled the anomalous, and, as they believed, temporary position of slaves, they spoke of "persons held to service," and in the three-fifths clause of "all other persons." They confided all power to "the people," and provided amply, as they believed, for the protection of the whole people. Thus in the second section of article one, they provided as follows for the organization of the House of Representatives:

"The House of Representatives shall be composed of members chosen every second year by *the people* of the several States, and the electors in each State shall have the qualifications requisite for electors of the most numerous branch of the State Legislature."

And in the amendments of the Constitution we see how careful they were at a later day to guard the rights of the people:

"ART. 1. Congress shall make no law respecting an establishment of religion, or prohibiting the free exercise thereof; or abridging the freedom of speech or of the press; or the right of *the people* peaceably to assemble and to petition the Government for a redress of grievances.

"ART. 2. A well-regulated militia being necessary to the security of a free State, the right of *the people* to keep and bear arms shall not be infringed."

"ART. 4. The right of *the people* to be secure in their persons, houses, papers, and effects, against unreasonable searches and seizures, shall not be violated."

"ART. 9. The enumeration in the Constitution of certain rights shall not be construed to deny or disparage others retained by *the people*.

"ART. 10. The powers not delegated to the United States by the Constitution, nor prohibited by it to the States, are reserved to the States respectively, or to *the people*."

It has, I know, been fashionable to deny that the framers of the Constitution intended to embrace colored persons when they used the word "people;" and it is still asserted by some that it was used with a mental reservation broad and effective enough to exclude them; but the Journals of the Convention and the general history of the times abound in contradictions of this false and mischievous theory, the source of all our present woes. A brief review of contemporaneous events ought to put this question at rest forever.

The Congress of the Confederation was in session on the 25th of June, 1778, the fourth of the Articles of Confederation being under consideration. The terms of the article as proposed were that "the free inhabitants of each of these States (paupers, vagabonds, and fugitives from justice excepted) shall be entitled to all privileges and immunities of free citizens in the several States." We learn by the Journal that "the delegates from South Carolina, being called on, moved the following amendment in behalf of their State: in article four, between the words 'free inhabitants' insert 'white.'" How was this proposition, identical with that now made to us, received by the sages there and then assembled? Eleven States voted on the question. Two, South Carolina being one of them, sustained the proposition; the vote of one State was divided; and eight, affirming the colored man's right to the privileges of citizenship, voted "no," and the proposition was thus negatived. South Carolina—then, as she has ever been, persistent in mischief—further moved, through her delegates, to amend by inserting after the words "the several States" the words "according to the law of such States respectively for the government of their own *free white* inhabitants." This proposition was also negatived by the same decisive vote, as appears by the Journal of the Congress of the Confederation, volume four, pages 379, 380. What two States did not vote upon the question the Journal does not indicate; but when it is remembered that Pennsylvania led her sisters in the great work of emancipation, and that it was not till nearly two years after that date that she abolished slavery, it will be seen that it was by a vote of slaveholders representing slave States, that the proposition to deny citizenship, its rights, privileges, and immunities, to the colored people was so emphatically rejected. The delegates could not, with propriety, have voted otherwise. To have done so, they would have agreed that, in violation of all comity, while they secured the rights of citizenship within the limits of their State to citizens of others, those other States might deny them to citizens of their own. They did not probably foresee that South Carolina might cast the shipwrecked citizen of another State who had been thrown upon her shores into a jail, because of the decree of the Almighty, who had given him a complexion not agreeable to the eyes of her people, and in default of the ability to pay jail fees thus unwillingly incurred, doom him and his posterity to the woes of perpetual slavery; but they did see that such a proposition opened the door to inequality, and possibly to oppression, and they resisted it with a firmness and forecast which their posterity have failed to honor or emulate.

Again, they could not have consistently voted for such a proposition; for, by the constitutions of their own States, free colored men were voters, and in the enjoyment of the rights of citizenship. Not only then, but in 1789, at the time of the adoption of the Constitution of the United States, there was but one State whose constitution distinguished in this respect against the colored man. This odious distinction, so fraught with unforeseen but terrible consequences, marred the constitution of South Carolina alone at the latter date.

The constitution of Massachusetts provided that

"Every male person (being twenty-one years of age, and resident in any particular town in this Commonwealth for the space of one year next preceding) having a freehold estate within the same town of the annual income of three pounds, or any estate of the value of sixty pounds, shall have a right to vote in the choice of a representative or representatives for the said town."

Rhode Island had adopted no constitution, but continued under colonial charter, which provided for the election of members of the General Assembly by "the major part of the freemen of the respective towns or places."

Connecticut also continued under colonial charter, according to which the qualifications of an elector were "maturity in years, quiet and peaceable behavior, a civil conversation, and forty shillings freehold, or forty pounds personal estate."

The constitution of New York provided that—

"Every male inhabitant of full age, who shall have personally resided within one of the counties of this State for six months immediately preceding the day of election, shall, at such election, be entitled to vote for representatives of the said county in the Assembly, if, during the time aforesaid, he shall have been a freeholder possessing a freehold of the value of twenty pounds within the said county, or have rented a tenement therein of the yearly value of forty shillings, and have rated and actually paid taxes to this State."

The constitution of New Jersey contained this provision:

"All inhabitants of this colony of full age, who are worth fifty pounds proclamation money clear estate in the same, and have resided within the county in which they claim to vote for twelve months immediately preceding the election, shall be entitled to vote for representatives in Council and Assembly, and also for all other public officers that shall be elected by the people of the county at large."

The constitution of Pennsylvania provided that—

"Every freeman of the full age of twenty-one years, having resided in this State for the space of one whole year next before the day of election for representatives, and paid public taxes during that time, shall enjoy the right of an elector; provided always that sons of freeholders of the age of twenty-one years shall be entitled to vote although they have not paid taxes."

The constitution of Delaware declared that—

"The right of suffrage in the election for members of both houses shall remain as exercised by law at present."

The declaration of rights, prefixed to the constitution, contained the following:

"Every freeman, having sufficient evidence of permanent common interest with and attachment to the community, hath a right of suffrage."

The constitution of Maryland provides that—

"All freemen, above twenty-one years of age, having a freehold of fifty acres of land in the county in which they offer to vote, and residing therein, and all freemen having property in this State above the value of thirty pounds current money, and having resided in the county in which they offer to vote one whole year next preceding the election, shall have a right of suffrage in the election of delegates for such county."

The constitution of Virginia contained a provision that—

"The right of suffrage in the election of members for both houses shall remain as exercised at present."

The declaration of rights, prefixed to the constitution, contained the following:

"All men having sufficient evidence of permanent common interest with and attachment to the community have the right of suffrage."

The constitution of North Carolina provided that—

"All freemen of the age of twenty-one years, who have been inhabitants of any one county within the State twelve months immediately preceding the day of any election, and shall have paid public taxes, shall be entitled to vote for members of the House of Commons for the county in which they reside."

The constitution of Georgia declared that—

"The electors of the members of both branches of the General Assembly shall be citizens and inhabitants of this State, and shall have attained to the age of twenty-one years, and have paid tax for the year preceding the election, and shall have resided six months within the county."

The constitution of South Carolina provided that—

"The qualifications of an elector shall be, every free *white* man, and no other person, who acknowledges the being of a God, and believes in a future state of rewards and punishments, and who has attained the age of one and twenty years, and hath been an inhabitant and resident in this State for the space of one whole year before the day appointed for the election he offers to give his vote at, and hath a freehold at least of fifty acres of land or a town lot, and hath been legally seized and possessed of the same at least six months previous to such election, or hath paid a tax the preceding year, or was taxable the present year, at least six months previous to the said election, in a sum equal to the tax on fifty acres of land, to the support of this government, shall be a person qualified to vote for, and shall be capable of electing, a representative or representatives."

But, Mr. Speaker, to evade the force of this overwhelming array of facts, the pro-slavery Democracy and purblind conservatism of the country have suggested that the thought of the black man was not present in the minds of those who fashioned these constitutions and bills of rights; that they could not have imagined that the freed slave or his posterity would have the audacity to ask that they should be recognized as freemen and citizens of our country; and with unblushing effrontery they have made the ignorant believe that the Government was organized, not for mankind, but for the white man alone. The falsity of these suggestions is fully exposed by the fact that South Carolina made the distinction, and in the Congress of the Confederation pressed it on the attention of the whole country, but will be still more amply demonstrated by the facts I shall hereafter cite. In every State but South Carolina, and possibly Virginia and Delaware, in which the right of suffrage was regulated by statute, and not by constitutional provision, the free colored man at that time was a voter. In no State constitution except that of South Carolina, which was replete with aristocratic provisions, was the right of suffrage limited by express terms to the white man; consequently but few, if any, of the members of the Convention that framed the Constitution of the United States could have failed to meet him as a voter at the polls. I remember well to have seen negroes at the polls exercising the right of suffrage in Pennsylvania, where they enjoyed it from the foundation of the government to the year 1838, when the growing influence of the increasing slave power of the country, operating on the political ambition of those whom the people had charged with no such duty, deprived colored men of this right by following the example of South Carolina and inserting the word "white" in the constitution of the State. Similar action restricted their right in New York, making it dependent on a property qualification, and deprived them of it in New Jersey and other States now free. To her praise be it spoken, except in Connecticut, which State, in 1817, in complaisance to South Carolina, inserted the word "white" in her constitution, they still enjoy the right throughout New England, not as a concession from men of modern days, but hereditarily, from the times in which the foundations of the Government were laid. Gentlemen around me from the State of Maryland doubtless well remember the days when the free colored man voted in their State. It was only in 1833 that he was deprived of that inestimable right by constitutional amendment within her limits. That the negro enjoyed this right in North Carolina until he was deprived of it in the same way is proven by the following extract from the opinion of Judge Gaston, of that State, in the State *vs.* Manuel, which was decided in 1838, and may be found in 4 Devereux and Battle's North Carolina Reports, page 25:

"It has been said that before our Revolution free persons of color did not exercise the right of voting for members of the colonial Legislature. How this may have been it would be difficult at this time to ascertain. It is certain, however, that very few, if any, could have claimed the right of suffrage for a reason of a very different character from the one supposed. The principle of freehold suffrage seems to have been brought over from England with the first colonists, and to have been preserved almost invariably in the colony ever afterward." * * * "The very Congress which framed our constitution [the State constitution of 1776] was chosen by freeholders. That constitution extended the elective franchise to every freeman who had arrived at the age of twenty-one and paid a public tax; and *it is a matter of universal notoriety that under it free persons, without regard to color, claimed and exercised the franchise until it was taken from free men of color a few years since by our amended constitution.*"

Tennessee was admitted to the Union in 1796. Her constitution provided as follows:

"Every freeman of the age of twenty-one years and upward, possessing a freehold in the county wherein he may vote, and being an inhabitant of this State, and *every freeman* being an inhabitant of any one county in the State six months immediately preceding the day of election, shall be entitled to vote for members of the General Assembly for the county in which he may reside."

This constitution, as will be seen, endured for forty years, during which the free colored men of the State enjoyed their political rights, and exercised, as will appear, a powerful and salutary influence upon public opinion and the course of legislation.

In 1834, a convention to revise that constitution assembled at Nashville, and, accepting the suggestion of South Carolina, by a vote of 33 to 23 limited the suffrage to free white men. During those forty years free negroes had enjoyed a right which made them a power; and no chapter in our history better illustrates the value of this power to both races, or how certainly great wrongs of this kind react and punish the wrong-doer. Cave Johnson is a name well known throughout the country and honored in Tennessee; and it was his boast that the free men of color gave his services to the country by electing him to Congress. On page 1305 of the Congressional Globe for the session of 1853-54, will be found the following statement of Hon. John Pettit, of Indiana, made in the United States Senate, May 25, 1854, while discussing the suffrage clause of the Kansas-Nebraska bill:

"Many of the States have conferred this right [of suffrage] upon Indians, and many, both North and South, have conferred it upon free negroes without property. Old Cave Johnson, of Tennessee, an honored and respectable gentleman, formerly Postmaster General, and for a long time a member of the other House, told me with his own lips that the first time he was elected to Congress from Tennessee (in 1828) it was by the votes of free negroes; and he told me how. Free negroes in Tennessee were then allowed by the constitution of the State to vote; and he was an iron manufacturer, and had a large number of free negroes as well as slaves in his employ. I well recollect the number he stated. One hundred and forty-four free negroes in his employ went to the ballot-box and elected him to Congress the first time he was elected."

Few will now deny that slavery is a curse alike to the master and the servile race. None will deny that slavery has been a curse to that State in view of the vast mineral resources of Tennessee; her fine natural sites for great cities; her capacity to feed, house, clothe, educate, and profitably employ free laborers; her recent history, the abundant source of future song and story; the pious and patriotic endurance of the brave and God-fearing people of the eastern section of the State, and the perfect abandon with which their more aristocratic fellow-citizens of the western section of the State espoused the cause of the rebellion; the cruelties inflicted on the loyal people by the traitors; the horrors and the heroism of the border warfare that has desolated her fair fields, and the rancorous feuds and intense hatreds, which the grave can only extinguish, that have been engendered among her people by the war. And who, if the apparently well-founded tradition be true, that a proposition to incorporate in her constitution of 1796 a clause prohibiting slavery was lost by a majority of one vote, will estimate the evil done by the man who thus decided that momentous question?

The history of slavery in Tennessee, and the determined resistance so long made against its struggles for supremacy, will, I am sure, justify a brief digression. There were in 1796, it is said, considerably less than five thousand slaves within her limits, who had been brought thither by the earlier settlers of what was then known as the territory south of the Ohio. The influence of the colored citizens is traceable throughout her earlier history. So early as 1801, before she had existed five years as a State, the Legislature conferred the power of emancipation upon the county courts of the State by an act, the preamble to which significantly says:

"Whereas the number of petitions presented to this Legislature praying the emancipation of slaves, not only tends to involve the State in great evils, but is also productive of great expense."

In 1812, the introduction of slaves into the State for sale was prohibited by law. Yet in the twenty years between 1790 and 1810, by the power of emigration from slave States and natural increase, the number swelled from less than four thousand to upward of forty-four thousand. This rapid increase of slave population alarmed the people, and emancipation societies were organized in different parts of the State. Extracts from an address delivered on the 17th of August, 1816, by request of one of these societies, and repeated with its approval on the 1st of January, 1817, and which, having been printed, not anonymously, but by Heiskell & Brown, was largely distributed by the society, are before me. It proposes to show,

First, the object or design of the society.

Second, that the principles of slavery are inconsistent with the laws of nature and revelation.

Third, some of its evils, both moral and political.

Fourth, that no solid objections lie against gradual emancipation.

To show the freedom with which the subject was then discussed, I offer a brief extract or two. In those days the people of America had not learned, nor did they yet pretend to believe, that the Constitution of the United States denied them the right to think of the condition of any class of suffering people, or made it a crime to utter their convictions and their philanthropic emotions. Thus this address to the people of Tennessee says:

"Slavery, as it exists among us, gives a master a property in the slaves and their descendants as much as law can give a property in land, cattle, goods, and chattels of any kind, to be used at the discretion of the master, or to be sold to whom, when, and where he pleases, with the descendants forever. It is true, if the master take away the life of the slave under certain circumstances, our laws pronounce it murder. But the laws leave it in the power of the master to destroy his life by a thousand acts of lingering cruelty. He may starve him to death by degrees, or he may whip him to death if he only take long enough time, or he may so unite the rigors of hard labor, stinted diet, and exposure as to shorten life. The laws watch against sudden murder, as if to leave the forlorn wretches exposed to any slow death that the cruelty and malignant passions of a savage may dictate. Nor is there any restraint but a sense of pecuniary loss, feeble barrier against the effects of the malevolent passions that are known to reside in the human heart. The most inhuman wretch may own slaves, as well as the humane and gentle. Should laws leave one human being in the power of another to such an extent? In many countries where slavery exists the laws prescribe the manner in which they shall be used, and that, too, in lands which do not boast either of the light and science we enjoy or of the liberty and equality which raise us above and distinguish us from all the nations of the globe."

Nor did the movement, as appears at least from this address, contemplate the abolition of slavery in Tennessee alone; for, after alluding to the great doctrines promulgated in the Declaration of Independence, it says:

"On the certainty of the unchangeableness of these truths, we justify our separation from the Government of Great Britain. For the defense and enjoyment of these principles our fathers willingly met death, and surrendered their lives martyrs. They bequeathed them to us as the greatest of human legacies. Yet slavery, as it exists in the United States, is in direct opposition to these self-evident maxims. Every line of our history, every battle in our struggle for independence, every anniversary of our national birth condemns the principles of slavery, and fixes on us the charge of glaring inconsistency; and every law passed by Legislatures in favor of slavery is in direct opposition to the principles of our national existence. Let us willingly do that which we justly blame Great Britain for refusing to do until forced, *namely, acknowledge the rights of men, and give, in a suitable way, more than one million and a half of people to enjoy these sacred rights.*"

In 1834, when the convention to revise the constitution assembled, the slaves in the State numbered more than one hundred and fifty thousand. The power of the slave oligarchy had increased, and opposition to the institution had perhaps become less powerful. But in the first week of the convention, petitions on the subject of emancipation were presented from the citizens of Maury county, and were soon followed by others from Robertson, Lincoln, Bedford, Overton, Roane, Rhea, Knox, Monroe, McMinn, Blount, Sevier, Cocke, Jefferson, Greene, and Washington, many of the signers being slaveholders, and all praying that all the slaves should be made free by the year 1866. By an unforeseen process, the prayer of those petitioners will be granted, though the convention to which they addressed their prayer gave an unfavorable response, and as if in derision of the petitioners, attempted to fasten his shackles more firmly on the slave. God, whose

"Ways seem dark, but, soon or late,
They touch the shining hills of day,"

in His infinite mercy and wisdom has in this respect reversed the decrees of man. Well for Tennessee and her bleeding people would it have been had the members of that convention bowed reverently to His will, as did the framers of the Constitution of the United States, and so worded the instrument they fashioned that it would not have informed posterity that so odious an institution as slavery had ever been tolerated by the State.

During the second week of the session, Matthew Stephenson, a farmer of Washington county, a native of Rockingham county, Virginia, moved "that a committee of thirteen, one from each congressional district, be appointed to take into consideration the propriety of designating some period from which slavery shall not be tolerated in this State, and that all memorials on that subject that have or may be presented to the convention be referred to said committee to consider and report thereon;" which resolution, by a vote of 38 to 20, was laid on the table on the 1st of January, 1835.

*

This action of the convention was not readily acquiesced in by the people; and to avert popular indignation it was "resolved that a committee of three, one from each division of the State, be appointed to draft the reasons that governed this convention in declining to act upon the memorials on the subject of slavery." The address prepared by the committee appointed under this resolution does not attempt to defend or apologize for slavery; does not deny that it is a great wrong; speaks of "the unenviable condition of the slave;" of slavery as "unlovely in all its aspects," and deplores "the bitter draught the slave is doomed to drink." It rests the defense of the convention on other grounds than divine sanction of this monstrous wrong, this hideous outrage upon every precept of Christianity, this violation of every clause of the decalogue. It puts its defense on the ground of policy, and asserts that a constitutional provision looking to gradual emancipation would deplete the State of its laborers; that men would hurry their slaves into Alabama, Mississippi, Louisiana, Missouri, or Arkansas, where they would be less kindly treated than in Tennessee, and where the prospect of ultimate emancipation would be more remote. This address to the people of Tennessee admonishes us of the perennial fountain of evil they would inflict on the people of the insurgent district, who would doom the more than three million six hundred and sixty-six thousand people of color, dwelling within its limits, to that dubious measure of freedom enjoyed by men to whom political rights are denied, by the following pointed passage:

"The condition of a free man of color, surrounded by persons of a different caste and complexion, is the most forlorn and wretched that can be imagined. He is a stranger in the land of his nativity; he is an outcast in the place of his residence; he has scarcely a motive to prompt him to virtuous action or to stimulate him to honorable exertions. At every turn and corner of the walks of life he is beset with temptations, strong, nay, almost irresistible, to the force of which in most cases he may be expected to yield, the consequence of which must be that he will be degraded, despised, and trampled upon by the rest of the community. When the free man of color is oppressed by the proud, or circumvented by the cunning, or betrayed by those in whom he has reposed confidence, do the laws of the land afford him more than a nominal protection? Denied his oath in a court of justice, unable to call any of his own color to be witnesses, if the injury he complains of has been committed by a white man, how many of his wrongs must remain unredressed; how many of his rights be violated with impunity; how poor a boon does he receive when he is receiving freedom, if what he receives can be called by that name. Unenviable as is the condition of the slave, unlovely as slavery is in all its aspects, bitter as the draught may be that the slave is doomed to drink, nevertheless his condition is better than the condition of the free man of color in the midst of a community of white men with whom he has no common interest, no fellow-feeling, no equality."

And it speaks to such with more pertinency than it did to those for whom it was written when it says:

"What, then, would be the condition of the community, with such a multitude of human beings turned loose in society, with all the habits, morals, and manners of the slave, *with only the name and nominal privileges, but without any of the real blessings of liberty or the real privileges of the freeman?* Would not two distinct classes of people in the same community array themselves against each other in perpetual hostility and mutual distrust? Would not the constant collision that would take place between them produce a feverish excitement, alike destructive to the happiness of both parties? Would not the condition of free people of color, under the operation of the causes already enumerated, be more wretched than the condition of the slaves? *Would not the white portion of the community be more insecure with such a multitude among them, who had no common interest with, no bond of union to, that part of the community with whom they were mixed, and yet from whom they were forever separated by a mark of distinction that time itself could not wear away?* The people of color, numerous as they would be, with no kindred feeling to unite them to that part of the community, whom they would both envy and hate, would nevertheless have at their command a portion of physical strength that might and probably would be wielded to the worst purposes. They would look across the southern boundary of the State, and there they would see in a state of servitude a people of their own color and kindred, to whom they were bound by the strong bonds of consanguinity, and with whom they could make a common cause, and would they not be strongly tempted to concert plans with them to exterminate the white man and take possession of the country? They would then possess the means of consulting together, of coöperating with each other, and *let it not be forgotten that they would be animated by every feeling of the human heart that impels to action.*"

Our millions will not look across the boundary and behold a people of their color and kindred in bondage. In all the States of Central America, as in Mexico, the colored man is not only free, but a citizen in the full enjoyment of all the rights accorded to any man under his Government. But on this point I shall have a few words to say hereafter.

How blinded by the pride of caste were the authors of the address from which I make these extracts! How fatally did they ignore the fact that God had made all nations of one blood! It was not necessary that Tennessee should expatriate her laborers, or maintain slavery, or create in her midst so dangerous a class. It was open to that convention to avoid the great iniquity which, it appears, a majority of its members had predetermined, namely, the deprivation of the free colored man of the political rights he had enjoyed for forty years, and to have maintained the existing rights of those whose labor was giving consideration to the State and wealth to its people. But they had already forgotten the maxims of the fathers; and it will be well if we do not adopt their folly as our wisdom. Let us profit by their sad experience, and be warned by the voice of Jefferson, who exclaimed:

"With what execration should the statesman be loaded, who, permitting one half the citizens thus to trample on the rights of the other, transforms those into despots and these into enemies—destroys the morals of the one part, and the *amor patriæ* of the other!"

And let us remember, too, that a wiser than he has said—

"Woe unto them that decree unrighteous decrees, and write grievousness which they have prescribed; to turn aside the needy from judgment, and take away the right from the poor."

But plausible as were the reasons set forth in this address, its authors did not intimate to the people that even they doubted that the great wrong of slavery would soon disappear; and, as appears by pages 92 and 93 of the Journal, they further said:

"But the friends of humanity need not despair; the memorialists need not dread that slavery will be perpetual in our highly-favored country." * * * * "Under the approving smile of Heaven, and the fostering care of

Providence, slavery will yet be extinguished in a way that will work no evil to the white man, while it produces the happiest effects upon the whole African race." * * * * "Let it be remembered that there is an appropriate *time for every work beneath the sun*, and a premature attempt to do any work, particularly any great work, seldom fails to prevent success. A premature attempt on the part of a sick man to leave his bed and his chamber would inevitably prolong his disease, or perhaps place it beyond the power of medicine. A similar attempt on the part of the poor man to place himself in a state of independence, by engaging in some plausible but imprudent speculation, would probably involve him in embarrassment from which he could not extricate himself throughout the whole remaining portion of his life. So a premature attempt on the part of the benevolent to get rid of the evils of slavery would certainly have the effect of postponing to a far distant day the accomplishment of an *event* devoutly and ardently desired by the wise and the good in every part of our beloved country."

The sophisms of this report were not permitted to pass without notice. Stout old Matthew Stephenson, (for he was then in the fifty-eighth year of his age,) sustained by several of his associates, caused their protest to be entered on the journals. They said, among other things:

"We believe the principles assumed in the report, and the arguments used in their support, are in their tendency subversive of the true principles of republicanism, and before we can consistently give them our unqualified assent we must renounce the doctrine that 'all men are created equal; that they are endowed by their Creator with certain unalienable rights; that among these are life, liberty, and the pursuit of happiness.' Above all, we believe the report is at variance with the spirit of the gospel, which is the glory of our land, the precepts and maxims of which are found in the Bible. One of its excellent rules is, 'As ye would that men should do unto you, do ye even so unto them.' Now, to apply this golden rule to the case of master and the slave, we have just to place each in the other's stead, then ask the question honestly, 'What would I that my servant, thus placed in power, should do unto me?'"

* * * * * * * * * * *

"But we are told nature has placed on the man of color a mark of distinction which neither time nor circumstances can obliterate.

"*We admit the fact, but are nevertheless unable to perceive in that a good reason for denying to them the common rights of man.* The words of eternal truth are, that God has made of one blood all nations that dwell upon the earth, and the undersigned, in the language of Cowper, are unwilling to 'find their fellow-creature guilty of a skin not colored like their own;' *nor can we admit as just the rule that would assign to men their rights according to the different shades of color.* In the opinion of the undersigned, all the evils so strikingly and so eloquently portrayed in the report, respecting the free people of color while among us, apply with equal, nay, with greater force to the same people while in slavery, unless, indeed, slavery gives dignity to man. And although the memorialists do not hint at retaining the *people of color* among us when free, but ask that some means be devised for their removal; nor would the undersigned be understood as advocating any system of emancipation unconnected with or without a view to their colonization; yet we believe they would be happier and safer subjects of our Government as free men than as slaves. *As we hold it wise policy in every Government to make it the interest of all its subjects to support, defend, and perpetuate its civil institutions, is it reasonable to suppose that any would desire the permanent existence of that Government which denied to them all the rights of freemen?* Solomon in his wisdom has said, 'Oppression makes a wise man mad.'"

Dr. Joseph Kincaid, of Bedford county, a native of Madison county, Kentucky, also prepared a protest against the doctrines of the address, and caused it to be entered on the Journals. From that protest I make but the following extract:

"Can the free man of color be torn from his wife and family and driven in chains to a foreign land and there sold in the market like a dumb brute to him who will give the greatest sum for him, though his heart bleeds and bosom yearns with bowels of compassion and paternal tenderness for the wife and children of his bosom, who are bone of his bone and flesh of his flesh? He cannot. Or can the children of the fond mother be torn from *her* bosom while her heart is wrung with distress, and she agonizes in despair and mourns for them, and will not be comforted, because they are not? This cannot be done. Then does this not *sweeten* the 'draught' which the free man of color daily drinks? Most indubitably it does. Are these blessings secured to the slave? We have seen they are not. What is it, then, which constitutes the situation of the slave *better* than that of the *free man of color?* Does the superior happiness and comfort of the slave over that of the free man of color consist in the amount of bread and meat which he receives at the hands of his master to subsist him, which he has not to trouble himself about the procuring of? The report seems to predicate a good portion of the solid comfort of the slave upon the daily rations which he draws from his master's stores. But this conclusion the undersigned cannot subscribe to; as an *American citizen* he would put a higher estimate upon the liberty which is enjoyed even by the free man of color. What! will it be said that *his* rights, privileges, and happiness shall be balanced in the scale against the allowance of coarse fare which is given for daily subsistence to the slave, and the tattered garments that are furnished him to defend his body against the inclemency of the season, and the chains with which he may be *bound* in order to send him to a foreign market? Monstrous doctrine! Cannot the free man of color, with the labor of his hands, one sixth part of his time, procure as ample a supply of food and raiment as is furnished the slave? Yea, and can he not then sit down under his own vine, in the bosom of his family, and enjoy it, and there shall 'be none to disturb or make him afraid?'"

Nor did the controversy end here; for the committee made a supplementary report, and true-hearted old Matthew Stephenson and his associates entered their second protest on the journal of the convention.

In drawing the picture of the condition of the free man of color, the committee representing the majority of the convention evidently had in view what they intended to make his future and not his past condition in that State; for the convention, instead of providing for the abolition of slavery, threw around that institution an additional safeguard by providing that "the General Assembly shall have no power to pass laws for the emancipation of slaves without the consent of their owner or owners;" and by a vote of 33 to 23 changed the language of the clause regulating the elective franchise from "freemen," as it had stood from the organization of the State, to "free white men," since which time the negro has had no voice or share in the management of the public affairs of that State. Thus South Carolina triumphed over freedom in Tennessee.

But to return to my line of argument, having wandered too far in this interesting digression.

Ample as this is, we do not depend on the action of the Congress of the Confederation, and of the Convention for framing the Constitution of the United States, and the provisions of the several State constitutions for all the proof the men of that period left that they recognized the right of man, by reason of his manhood, to the enjoyment of all the rights of citizenship. A long and uniform course of legislation relating to and regulating territory stretching from the lakes southward to the Gulf of Mexico, confirms the fact. Congress, under the Articles of Confederation, twice provided for the government of Territories, and under our present Constitution the Congress of the United States much more frequently. The distinguished men who occupied seats in those bodies prior to 1812 had not been enlightened by the sibylline mysteries given to the world in the celebrated letter of General Cass to Mr. Nicholson, nor by the doctrine of "popular sovereignty" so persistently reiterated by Douglas as his "great doctrine;" nor by Calhoun's theory, which was finally accepted as the cardinal, if not the sole doctrine of Democratic faith, that the flag of the United States, wherever it may be borne, on land or sea, carries with it and protects human slavery, as announced by Toombs in his Boston address of January 24, 1856. They knew that it was the duty of Congress, alike under the Articles of Confederation and the Constitution of the United States, to legislate for the Territories and provide governments for their regulation. The resolutions of the Congress of the Confederation for the temporary government of territory ceded by the individual States to the United States, adopted April 23, 1784, provided for the establishment of territorial governments by the "free males of full age;" and the famous Ordinance of July 13, 1787, for the government of the territory northwest of the river Ohio, which repeals the resolutions of 1784, and the salient point of which was known first as the "Jefferson proviso," and later, in connection with the Oregon struggle, as the "Wilmot proviso," vested the right of suffrage in the "free male inhabitants of full age," with a certain freehold qualification. This Ordinance was reënacted immediately after the adoption of our present Constitution, by the act of Congress of August 7, 1789; and in this respect was the precedent for every subsequent territorial act passed until 1812. The several acts passed from the foundation of the Government to that date, were as follows:

Under the Congress of the Confederation, those to which I have referred, namely, that of April 23, 1784, "for the temporary government of territory ceded or to be ceded by the individual States to the United States;" and that of July 13, 1787, "for the government of the territory of the United States northwest of the river Ohio."

And by the Congress of the United States since the adoption of the Constitution:

The act of August 7, 1789, already referred to as reënacting the Ordinance of 1787;

The act of May 26, 1790, for the government of the territory of the United States south of the river Ohio, under which, as we have seen, the State of Tennessee was organized;

The act of April 7, 1798, for the establishment of a government in the Mississippi territory;

The act of May 7, 1800, establishing Indiana Territory;

The act of March 26, 1804, for the government of Louisiana, which provided for a legislative council, to be appointed by the President of the United States, and not for an elective Legislature, as did all the rest;

The act of January 11, 1805, for the government of Michigan Territory;

The act of March 2, 1805, for the establishment of the Territory of Orleans; and

The act of February 3, 1809, for the government of Illinois Territory.

And in no one of these ten acts was any restriction placed on the right of suffrage by reason of the color of the citizen. In none of them was the word "white" used to limit the right to suffrage.

The next territorial act was that of June 4, 1812, providing for the government of Missouri Territory. More than twenty-two years had then passed since the adoption of the Constitution; and the men who had achieved our independence and fashioned our institutions in harmony with the fundamental truths they had declared, and who during this long period, more than the average active life of a generation, had resisted the aristocratic and strife-engendering demands of South Carolina, were rapidly passing, indeed most of them had passed, from participation in public affairs. Meanwhile, slavery had been strengthened by the unhappy compromise of the Constitution conceded to South Carolina and Georgia, by which "the migration or importation of such *persons* as any of the States now existing shall think proper to admit" was permitted for the period of twenty years. Meanwhile, too, the people of the country, enjoying unmeasured and unanticipated prosperity, forgot that "eternal vigilance is the price of liberty," and that "power is ever stealing from the many to the few;" and proud of their own achievements began to look with contempt upon the ignorant laborers they owned or employed, and their kindred newly imported from the coast of Africa; and began that long and rapid series of concessions to the fell spirit of slavery which made the present war inevitable, if free labor and the doctrine of a fair day's wages for a fair day's work were to be maintained in any part of the country. In the adoption of the territorial bill of 1812, South Carolina and slavery triumphed over freedom and the more powerful North, and the word "white," rejected in 1778 and thenceforth, was now inserted in the clause regulating suffrage in the fundamental law of a Territory.

Successful resistance to that innovation on well-established precedent would have secured freedom to Missouri, and in all probability averted the border wars of Kansas and the grander controversy in which we are engaged, and of which the Kansas feuds were but the sure precursor.

Can any candid man, in the face of this mass of concurrent evidence, assert that the fathers of our Government found in the fact of color cause for the denial of citizenship and the exercise of suffrage to any freeman? But more and if possible more pregnant proof on the point exists: not only did they assert the right of negroes to suffrage by rejecting the proposition of South Carolina in the Congress for framing Articles of Confederation, and protect it by the Constitution of the United States, and confirm it by twelve territorial laws; but, as I shall proceed to show, they by express treaty stipulation, first with France and again with Spain, guarantied them "the enjoyment of all the rights, advantages, and immunities of citizens of the United States," and the "free enjoyment of their liberty, property, and the religion which they professed." To show how unqualifiedly this was done under the administration of Mr. Jefferson, I beg leave to read a brief extract from that most interesting and instructive pamphlet, "The Emancipated Slave Face to Face with his Old Master," by J. McKaye, special commissioner from the War Department to the valley of the lower Mississippi, and also a member of the Freedmen's Inquiry Commission:

"The valley of the lower Mississippi, from an early period of its settlement, contained a proportionately large free colored population. In 1803, when the territory of which the State of Louisiana forms a part, was ceded by the French republic to the United States, these free colored men were already quite numerous, and many of them were possessed of considerable property. They were not only as free as any other portion of the population, but in general as well educated and intelligent. Many of them were the children of the early white settlers, and had always enjoyed a certain social as well as civil equality. As to the enjoyment of political rights under the old Spanish and French régimes, neither white nor black settlers ever had much experience; consequently there had never arisen among them much question of these rights, or as to whom they belonged. The French republic, founded on 'liberty, equality, fraternity,' had not yet quite forgotten the import of these words, and hence caused to be inserted in the treaty of cession a solemn stipulation in the words following, to wit:

"'ART. 3. The inhabitants of the ceded territory shall be incorporated into the Union of the United States, and admitted as soon as possible, according to the principles of the Federal Constitution, to the enjoyment of all the rights, advantages, and immunities of citizens of the United States; and in the mean time they shall be maintained and protected in the free enjoyment of their liberty, property, and the religion which they profess.'"

The Floridas, though less populous than the Louisiana territory, had quite as large a proportionate part of negroes and mulattoes among their population. By the treaty of February 22, 1819, with Spain, she ceded to the United States "all the territories which belong to her, situated to the eastward of the Mississippi, known by the name of East and West Floridas." The sixth article of the treaty is as follows:

"The inhabitants of the territories which his Catholic Majesty cedes to the United States by treaty shall be incorporated in the Union of the United States as soon as may be consistent with the principles of the Federal Constitution, and admitted to the enjoyment of all the privileges, rights, and immunities of the citizens of the United States."

My proposition is that the Government of the United States was instituted to secure the rights of all the citizens of the country, and not for the benefit of men of one race only, and I know not where to look for evidence that would strengthen the conclusiveness of the mass of proof I have thus adduced, embracing as it does the action of the framers of all the State constitutions but one, of the Congress for framing Articles of Confederation, of the Convention for framing the Constitution of the United States, the acts of Congress in unbroken series throughout the active life of a generation, and the solemn obligations assumed by the executive department of the national Government in the exercise of the treaty-making power. If other source of proof there be it can only serve to make assurance doubly sure.

Mr. Speaker, it is safe to assert that in every State, save South Carolina, and possibly Virginia and Delaware—in which two States the question of suffrage was regulated by statute and not by constitutional provision—negroes participated in constituting the Convention which framed the Constitution of the United States, and voted for members of the State conventions to which the question of its ratification was submitted; and as that Constitution contains no clause which expressly or by implication deprives them of the protecting power and influence of the instrument they participated in creating, I may well say that to secure internal peace by the establishment of political homogeneity, and perpetuate it by the abolition of political classes and castes whose conflicting rights and interests will provoke incessant agitation, and ever and anon, as the oppressed may be inspired by the fundamental principles of our Government, or goaded by wrongs excite armed insurrection, we need adopt no new theory, but accept the principles of our fathers, and administer in good faith to all men the institutions they founded on them.

As a step to this, my amendment proposes, not that the entire mass of people of African descent, whom our laws and customs have degraded and brutalized, shall be immediately clothed with all the rights of citizenship. It proposes only to grant the right of suffrage, inestimable to all men, to those who may be so far fitted by education for its judicious exercise as to be able to read the Constitution and laws of the country, in addition to the brave men, who, in the name of law and liberty, and in the hope of leaving their children heirs to both, have welcomed the baptism of battle in the naval and military service of the United States, and who are embraced by the amendment reported by the committee. This, I admit, will be an entering wedge, by the aid of which, in a brief time, the whole mass improved, enriched, and enlightened by the fast-coming and beneficent providences of God, will be qualified for and permitted to enjoy those rights by which they may protect themselves and aid in giving to all others that near approach to exact justice which we hope to attain from the intelligent exercise of universal suffrage and the submission of all trials of law in which a citizen may be interested to the decision of his peers as jurors.

I am, Mr. Speaker, under but one specific pledge to my constituents other than that which promised to vote away the last dollar from each man's coffer and the last able-bodied son from his hearthside, if they should be needed for the effectual suppression of the rebellion, and that is, that I will in their behalf consent to no proposed system of reconstruction which shall place the loyal men of the insurrectionary district under the unbridled control of the wicked and heartless traitors who have involved us in this war, and illustrated their barbarity by the fiendish cruelties they have practiced on their loyal neighbors, negro soldiers and unhappy prisoners of war; and to that pledge, God helping me, I mean to prove faithful. The future peace and prosperity of the country demand this much at our hands. The logic of our institutions, the principles of the men who achieved our independence and who framed those institutions, alike impel us to this course, as necessary as it will be wise and just.

Let us meet the question fairly. Do our institutions rest on complexional differences? Can we cement and perpetuate them by surrendering the patriots of the insurgent district, shorn of all political power, into the hands of the traitors whom we propose to propitiate by such a sacrifice of faith and honor? Did God ordain our country for a single race of men? Is there reason why the intelligent, wealthy, loyal man of color shall stand apart, abased, on election day, while his ignorant, intemperate, vicious, and disloyal white neighbor participates in making laws for his government? What is the logic that denies to a son the right to vote with or against his father, because it has pleased Heaven that he should partake more largely of his mother's than of that father's complexion? And is it not known to all of us that well-nigh forty per cent. of the colored people of the South are children of white fathers, who, after we subjugate them, will with professions of loyalty only lip deep, enjoy the right of suffrage in the reconstructed States? Shall he, though black as ebony be his skin, who, by patient industry, obedience to the laws, and unvarying good habits, has accumulated property on which he cheerfully pays taxes, be denied the right of a voice in the government of a State to whose support and welfare he thus contributes, while the idle, reckless, thriftless man of fairer complexion shall vote away his earnings and trifle with his life or interests as a juror? Shall the brave man who has periled life, and mayhap lost limb, who has endured the dangers of the march, the camp, and the bivouac in defense of our Constitution and laws, be denied their protection, while the traitors in the conquest of whom he assisted enjoy those rights, and use them as instruments for his oppression and degradation? Shall he who, in the language of my amendment, may be able to read the Constitution of the United States, and who finds his pleasure in the study of history and political philosophy, whose integrity is undoubted, whose means are ample, be voiceless in the councils of the nation, and read only to learn that the people of free and enlightened America, among whom his lot has been cast, sustain the only Government which punishes a race because God in His providence gave it a complexion which its unhappy members would not have accepted had it been submitted to their choice or volition? And can he who will answer these questions affirmatively believe that Governments are instituted among men to secure their rights, that they derive their powers from the consent of the governed, and that it is the duty of a people, when any Government becomes destructive of their rights, to alter or abolish it, and establish a new Government? Sir, our hope for peace, while we attempt to govern two fifths of the people of one half of our country in violation of these fundamental principles, will be idle as the breeze of summer or the dreams of the opium eater.

In this connection let me call the attention of the House to a fact to which I have already invited that of many members and other distinguished gentlemen. By the census of 1860 it appears that South Carolina had but 291,300 white inhabitants, and 412,408 colored. Among the former we have no reason to know or believe that, since the death of Pettigrew, there is a single loyal man; while the latter, we have no reason to doubt, are all as loyal as Robert Small, the patriot pilot of Charleston harbor. Are we to declare that one white citizen of South Carolina is entitled to more weight in the councils of the nation than two citizens of a northern State; and are the 291,300 to be vested with the absolute government of 703,708? Is the entire loyalty of that State to be confided to the tender mercies of the chagrined and humiliated, but unconverted and devilish traitors of the State that engendered and inaugurated this bloody rebellion? And shall they who have fought for our flag, sheltered our soldiers when flying from loathsome prisons, guided them through hidden paths by night, saving them from starvation by sharing with them their poor and scanty food, and whose unceasing prayer to God has been for our triumph, be handed over to the lash, the iron collar, and the teeth of the blood-hound, to gratify our pride of race and propitiate our malignant foes?

Again, the census shows that Mississippi, in 1860 had but 350,901 white inhabitants, and 437,404 colored. Disloyalty was almost as prevalent among the white men of Mississippi as among those of South Carolina. But who has heard from traveler, correspondent, returning soldier, or other person, that he has found a colored traitor within the limits of that State? And shall we, ignoring our theory that "Governments derive their just powers from the consent of the governed," say to the majority in these States, "Stand back! time and labor cannot qualify you to take care of yourselves? We spurn you for the service you have rendered our cause, and hand you over to the degradation, the unrequited toil, the slow but sure and cruel extermination which your oppressors in their pride and madness will provide for you?"

And mark you, Mr. Speaker, again, how nearly the races are balanced in Louisiana, Georgia, and Alabama. In Louisiana there are 357,456 whites and 350,546 colored people. Of whites in Georgia there are 591,550, and of colored people there are 465,736. In Alabama the whites number 526,271, while there are of colored 437,930. And in Florida there is the same near approach to equality of numbers, the white population being 77,747 and the colored 62,677. Are these people by our decree to remain dumb and voiceless in freedom? They are no longer slaves. War and the high prerogative of the President, called into exercise by the war, have made them free. Will you inflict upon them all the miseries predicted for the free colored people of Tennessee in the extract which I have read to you? No, rather let us bind them to our Government by enabling them to protect their interests, share its power, and appreciate its beneficence. This we can do, and the alternative is to so degrade them that they will prove an annoyance and an object of distrust to their white neighbors, an element of weakness to the Government, and a constant invitation to diplomatic intrigue and war by the ambitious man who dreams of a Latin empire in America, and who, following the example of the States of Central and South America, will accept the descendant of Africa as a Basque and a citizen of his proposed empire.

And here it may not be amiss to pause for a moment and contemplate some ulterior consequences of our action on this subject. Trained in the school of Democracy, I am a believer in the "manifest destiny" of my country. Having regarded the acquisition by Mr. Jefferson of the Louisiana territory as wise and beneficent, though unwarranted by the Constitution, beholding great advantages in the acquisition of Florida, and having believed that, without war, could we have patiently waited, Texas would have come to us naturally as a State or States of the Union, I am used to dreaming of the just influence the United States are to exercise, from end to end of the American continent. Among the most ephemeral products of our era will be the Franco-Austrian empire in Mexico, if we be but true to our own principles in this season of doubt and perplexity. Our infidelity to principles alone can give it perpetuity. Within its limits the question of color is not a political or a social question; it is purely one of taste. There, as in Central and South America, the colored man is a freeman. And we are to determine whether the sympathies of these millions of people within our own borders are to be with the Government whose supremacy they have aided in reëstablishing or with the wily and ambitious man who will pledge them citizenship on condition that they aid him in carrying the limits of his Latin empire to the northern boundary of the Gulf States of America. To them the United States or Mexico will be the exemplar nation of the world. Before her ruder laws all men are equal. Let ours be not less broad and just.

The tropical and malarious regions of Central America have, during the prevalence of slavery, seemed to be the natural geographical boundary of our influence in that direction. Tropical regions are not the home of the white man. They were not made for him. God did not adapt him to them. They are prolific in wealth, invite to commercial intercourse, yield many things necessary to the success of our arts and industry, and will one day afford a market for immense masses of our productions. But we cannot occupy them; we cannot develop their resources. Nor can the negro, in the ignorance and degradation to which we have hitherto doomed him. We have at length made him a soldier, and if need be he will carry our arms and our flag triumphantly over that to us pestilential region; and, if we make him a citizen; open to his children the school-house; give him the privilege of the workshop, the studio, the hall of science; admit him to the delights and inspirations of literature, philosophy, poetry—in brief, if we recognize him as a man and open to him the broad fields of American enterprise and culture, he will see that nature has given him the monopoly of the wealth of that region, and will bless the world by making himself the master of it. By this means, and this alone, can we extend our influence over that region, and prepare for the ultimate Americanization of those drained by the Orinoko, the Amazon, and the Parana. As a citizen, nature will prompt the colored man to achieve these grand results. But if we leave the race a disfranchised and disaffected class in our midst, numbering millions, and embracing hundreds of thousands of men who in pursuit of freedom have bared their breasts to the storm of battle, and who are no longer debarred by statute from access to the sources of thought and knowledge, they will, let me reiterate the fact, be a ready and powerful ally to any power that may be disposed to disturb our peace and that will promise them the enjoyment of the rights of men as accorded to every citizen by its Government.

But it may be said, "history vindicates your theory; our fathers did mean that the black man should be a citizen and a voter; to deny him his rights is illogical as you have suggested; it would be better to secure his loyalty to the Government by its even-handed justice, but such an act would exasperate the southern people, and we do not think it wise to do that; his race is inferior; and, in short, we will not do it." Who says his race is inferior? Upon what theater have you permitted him to exhibit or develop his power? Give him an opportunity to exhibit his capacity, and let those who follow you and have before them the results he produces in freedom judge as to his relative position in the scale of human power and worth. To whom and to what do you say the American negro and mulatto are inferior? Was our Government fashioned for the Caucasian alone? Will you, as Theodore Tilton well asked, exchange the negro for the Esquimaux, for the Pacific islander, for the South American tribes? Will you exchange our negroes for so many Mongolians, Ethiopians, American Indians, or Malays? I apprehend that the universal answer to these questions will be in the negative; because, oppress them as we may, we rate the American negroes as next to our own proud race in the scale of humanity. And shall we erect around our civilization, our privileges, and immunities, a more than Chinese wall? Shall America, proud of her democracy, become the most exclusive of all nations of the world? Or shall she carry her faith into her life and become the home of mankind, the empire of freedom, and, by her example, the reformer of the world?

Let us frankly accept Jefferson's test as to the right of suffrage, and give it practical effect. In a letter dated July 12, 1816, in discussing a proposed amendment to the constitution of Virginia, Mr. Jefferson said:

"The true foundation of republican government is the equal right of every citizen in his person and property, and in their management. Try by this as a tally every provision of our constitution and see if it hangs directly on the will of the people. Reduce your Legislature to a convenient number for full but orderly discussion. *Let every man who fights or pays exercise his just and equal right in their election.*"—*Jefferson's Works*, vol. 7, page 11.

And again, in a letter written April 19, 1824, he said:

"However nature may, by mental or physical disqualifications, have marked infants and the weaker sex for the protection rather than the direction of Government, yet *among men who either pay or fight for their country no line of right can be drawn.*"—*Works*, vol. 7, page 345.

And again, as if to show how well considered his opinion was, in the Notes on Virginia, speaking of the then constitution of that State, he said:

"This constitution was formed when we were new and inexperienced in the science of government. It was the first, too, that was formed in the whole United States. No wonder, then, that time and trial have discovered very capital defects in it:

"1. The majority of the men in the State *who pay and*

fight for its support are unrepresented in the Legislature, the roll of freeholders entitled to vote, not including generally the half of the militia or of the tax-gatherers."—*Works*, vol. 8, page 359.

By adopting this sound test, which, be it remembered, was the only one recognized by the fathers, and adhering to it, our practice will harmonize with our theories, and the repugnance between the races will gradually disappear. Wealth and power conceal many deformities, and will make the black man less odious to all than he now seems. Thus will consistent adherence to principle give strength and peace to our country.

But if, on the other hand, we ignore the rights of these four million people and their posterity, the demon of agitation will haunt us in the future fearfully as it has in the past. The appeals of these millions for justice will not go forth in vain; and the liberal, the conscientious, the philanthropic, the religious, now that our Christian church recognizes her long off-cast child philanthropy, will be found in hostile array against what the commercial and planting interests will regard as the conservatism of the day; and though we find that we have buried the slavery question, our peace will be disturbed by the negro question constantly, and fearfully as it has been by the struggle between slavery and free labor. To which party ultimate victory would be vouchsafed in such a controversy I need not ask, as the nation acknowledges that God still lives and is omnipotent.

Again, such action is necessary to prevent the reëstablishment of our old tormentor, slavery. It is hoped that the proposed amendment to the Constitution, forever prohibiting slavery, may be adopted. But it has not yet passed this House; and if it had, who can guaranty its adoption by three fourths of the State Legislatures? I hope and believe that that amendment will be adopted; but it is within the range of possibility that it may be defeated. And how, in that event, save by the suffrage of the colored man, by his right to protect himself, his power at the ballot-box, shall we prevent his subjugation, or the bloody war that such an attempt might provoke—the reënactment on the broader theater of our southern States of the terrible tragedies that ensued upon the attempt to again reduce to bondage the freed slaves of St. Domingo?

Let it be borne in mind that States within the Union determine through their organism who shall be citizens and under what condition the people may enjoy their rights, and that, if the proposed amendment to the Constitution fail by want of the approval of a sufficient number of the State Legislatures, and South Carolina, when readmitted should determine to reënslave her freed men, and they should resist by force, although they constitute so largely the majority of her people, it would be the duty of the Government to bring the naval and military power of the United States into action in support of the authority of the State, as it did to suppress the Dorr rebellion in Rhode Island and repel the invasion of Virginia by John Brown and his twenty-two undisciplined volunteers.

But gentlemen may say that we need not fear such an effort as this; that the humanity of the age will prevent it. The humanity of the age has not prevented similar outrages. Neither the humanity of the age, nor the prudence of the people of the South, nor their sense of justice, nor their love of country prevented a bloody war for the purpose of overthrowing democratic institutions and founding an empire, the corner-stone of which should be human slavery. Let us not, therefore, while it is in our power to embody justice in laws and constitutions, be content to rely upon man's abstract sense of justice or his love for his fellow-man. Every gentleman knows that it has been the usage of every slave State to reduce free men, women, and children to bondage. Did not New Jersey, so late as 1797—as appears from the State *vs.* Waggoner, 1 Halstead's Reports—hold that American Indians might be reduced to and held in slavery? Has it not been lawful in Virginia, as appears by her Revised Code and the Constitution of 1851, to apprehend and sell, by the overseers of the poor, "for the benefit of the LITERARY FUND," any emancipated slave that might remain within the State more than twelve months after his or her right to freedom had accrued? Has not South Carolina sold free colored citizens of Massachusetts into bondage, because she had torn them from the vessels on which they had entered her ports, imprisoned them and brought them, though accused of no criminal offense, under charges for jail fees which she had deprived them of the means of paying? And has not North Carolina, under her act of 1741, been in the habit of dooming to slavery the unoffending offspring of any white woman-servant and a negro, mulatto or Indian. How horrible must have been the crime of the infant born of a *white* mother and an *Indian* father that it should thus, by special statutory provision, be punished by life-long, unrequited servitude, and be made the progenitor of a race of slaves. How dark indeed must have been the African blood of the child whose mother was a white woman and whose father an American Indian!

I know not that the books, full as they are of such instances, furnish any more absolute illustration of the power of a State over its people than this. And yet other and grander illustrations of that power on this and cognate questions rush upon my memory. But a few years since, it was gravely proposed by the Legislature of Maryland to expel from the limits of that State some eighty thousand people, because they were of African descent. The act passed both branches of the Legislature and was referred to the people for popular sanction. And the main argument by which the proposition was defeated at the polls was the selfish one that the land of the white citizen would remain untilled if these laborers were driven from their homes. Had it been determined otherwise, the people or the Government of the United States could not have prevented the execution of the infamous decree, but could have been called to enforce it. A similar proposition, at a later date, found favor in Tennessee; but the lingering spirit of her earlier settlers rejected it upon the simple and higher ground of humanity. Yet had such a law been enacted, and had the free people of color resisted it with force, did not we and every man in the North stand pledged to sustain the Government in the use of the naval and military power in carrying it into execution? Dorr's rebellion, and the manner in which the United States Government suppressed it, have a place in the history of our country, and illustrate the working of our system of Government.

But why speak of unsuccessful propositions, about which perverse ingenuity may raise questions? Surely we have not forgotten the act by which the State of Arkansas summarily decreed the banishment of free negroes and mulattoes who had their homes in that State, and the enslavement of all such as might not be able to make their escape within the brief time allowed for the purpose. They numbered many thousands. Some of them had been given freedom by their fathers, whose lingering humanity would not permit them to sell the children of their loins. Others had earned their freedom by honest toil, by acts of patriotism, or by deeds of generous philanthropy, the requital of which had been the bestowal of the poor measure of liberty that the free negro might enjoy within the limits of that State. The act to which I refer is No. 151 of the acts of the General Assembly of the State of Arkansas for the session of 1858-59, and may be found on page 175 of the pamphlet laws of that session. It was approved February 12, 1859, and contains twelve sections. Time will not permit me to cite the whole of this iniquitous statute; but two sections I must give entire. Section first is as follows:

"*Be it enacted by the General Assembly of the State of Arkansas,* That no free negro or mulatto shall be permitted to reside within the limits of this State after the 1st day of January, A. D. 1860."

And the tenth section reads thus:

"*Be it further enacted,* That it shall not be lawful for any person hereafter to emancipate any slave in this State."

Could language or rhetoric give force and amplitude to these provisions? The intermediate sections provide for the arrest and sale of any free negro or mulatto over the age of twenty-one years who might be found within the limits of the State after the date indicated in the first section, and the disposition to be made of the funds arising from their sale. As a bribe to the people of the several counties of the State to see the law faithfully executed, the surplus of each sale, after deducting the costs, was to be paid into the county treasury. They provided also for the hiring of those free colored persons who were not twenty-one years of age, and for the sale of such of these hirelings as might be found within the limits of the State thirty days after the expiration of their term of service. When it is remembered that, by a reversal of the immemorial and universal presumption that man is free, it had been provided in this and all other slave States that the presumption that he was a slave arose from the fact that any measure of African blood flowed in a man's veins, and that it was the duty, not only of police and other officers, but of every citizen who found a person of African descent at large to arrest him and demand the evidence of his freedom, and, in default of the production thereof, to cast him into jail, and that for the jail fees thus accruing he might be sold, it will be seen how impossible it was for these poor and illiterate people to make their exit from that State and through those coterminous to it whose laws contained the same barbarous provisions.

The humanity of the act is embodied in the eleventh section, which provides for the support of "children under the age of seven years who have no mothers, and who cannot be put out for their food and clothing," and for "the aged and infirm negroes and mulattoes who may be ascertained to be incapable of leaving the State, *or cannot be sold* after being apprehended." Less merciful than Herod, the citizens of Arkansas did not slay all these innocent children, but with wise regard to the future welfare of the treasury of each county, having deprived them of the support their natural guardians and fond parents could and would have provided them, and having torn from the aged and infirm who were incapable of leaving the State, and "could not be sold," the stout sons or gentle daughters whose years would have been gladdened by toiling to sustain those weary and aged ones in their declining years, they made it the duty of the county courts to make provision out of the proceeds of the sale of the able-bodied for the support of those who they thus robbed of their natural support and protection, leaving the aged and infirm to travel rapidly toward paupers' graves, and the children to be sold into slavery as cupidity might bring purchasers to the almshouse. Let men no longer speak of the laws of Draco, but say that an American State has, in the infernal inhumanity of her legislation, exceeded in cruelty the despots of all nations and all ages. Had the colored people of Arkansas had the right of suffrage their party influence would have saved us the shame we feel as we contemplate this page of American history.

The possible repetition of such acts as these by the aristocracy of the old States, when they shall again be fairly in the Union, is not matter of speculation. The purpose is already avowed. I have myself heard it said by men, now professedly loyal, that the condition of the negro will be made more horrible as freemen than it has ever been in slavery; and they have said to me, "You know that where the laborers are ignorant and powerless, as these will be, the will of the employer is their supreme law."

Among the witnesses examined by the freedmen's inquiry commission was Colonel George H. Hanks, of the fifteenth regiment Corps d'Afrique, member of the Board of Enrollment, and superintendent of negro labor in the department of the Gulf. Colonel Hanks went to Louisiana as a lieutenant in the twelfth Connecticut volunteers, under General Butler, and was appointed superintendent of the contrabands under General Sherman. His testimony illustrates the fitness of the colored people for freedom, and proves the determination of their old masters that they shall never, by their consent, enjoy it. Thus he says:

"The negroes came in scarred, wounded, and some with iron collars round their necks. I set them at work on abandoned plantations, and on the fortifications. At one time we had six thousand five hundred of them; there was not the slightest difficulty with them. They are more willing to work, and more patient than any set of human beings I ever saw. It is true there is a general dislike to return to their old masters; and those who have remained at home are suspicious of foul play, and feel it to be necessary to run away to test their freedom. This year the dislike has very much lessened; they begin to feel themselves more secure, and do not hesitate to return for wages. The negroes *willingly accept the condition of labor for their own maintenance, and the musket for their freedom.* I knew a family of five who were freed by the voluntary enlistment of one of the boys. He entered the ranks for the avowed purpose of freeing his family. His name was Moore; he was owned by the Messrs. Leeds, iron founders; they resided within one of the parishes excepted in the proclamation of emancipation. He was the first man to fall at Pascagoula. Upon starting he said to his family 'I know I shall fall, but you will be free.'

"A negro soldier demanded his children at my hands. I wanted to test his affection. I said 'they had a good home.' He said, 'Lieutenant, I want to send my children to school; my wife is not allowed to see them; I am in your service; I wear military clothes; I have been in three battles; I was in the assault at Port Hudson; I want my children; they are my flesh and blood.'"

Again:

"The colored people manifest the greatest anxiety to educate their children, and they thoroughly appreciate the benefits of education. I have known a family to go with two meals a day in order to save fifty cents a week to pay an indifferent teacher for their children."

After having spent nearly two years in daily intercourse with the planters in the department of the Gulf, Colonel Hanks, in his sworn testimony, says:

"Although they begin to see that slavery is dead, yet the spirit of slavery still lives among them. Many of them are even more rampant to enslave the negro than ever before. They make great endeavors to recover *what they call their own negroes.* One planter offered me $5,000 to return his negroes. They have even hired men to steal them from my own camp. (The old spirit still prompting to the old crime, which long ago was declared felony by the law of nations, if perpetrated in Africa.)" * * * *

"They yield to the idea of freedom only under compulsion. They submit to the terms dictated by the Government because obliged so to do. Mr. V. B. Marmillon, one of the richest and most extensive sugar planters in the whole valley of the Mississippi, took the oath of allegiance, but refused to work his own plantation unless he could have *his own negroes* returned to him. He had fourteen hundred and fifty acres of cane under cultivation; his whole family of plantation hands left him and came to New Orleans, reporting themselves to me. Among them could be found every species of mechanic and artisan. I called them up and informed them that the Government had taken possession of old master's crop, and that they were needed to take it off, and would be paid for their labor. All consented to return; but next morning when the time came for their departure, not one would go. One of them said, 'I will go anywhere else to work, but you may shoot me before I will return to the old plantation.' I afterwards ascertained that Marmillon, whom they called 'Old Cotton Beard,' had boasted in the presence of two colored girls, house servants, how he would serve them when he once more had them in his power. These girls had walked more than thirty miles in the night to bring this information to their friends."

Colonel Hanks adds:

"It is undoubtedly true that this year a change for the better seems to be taking place. In some parishes the letting of plantations to northern men has a powerful effect. The disposition of the planters, however, toward their old slaves, when they consent to hire them, is by no means friendly. I told a planter recently that it was the express order of General Banks that the negroes should be educated. He replied that 'no one should teach his negroes.'"

And he further declares it as his deliberate judgment that—

"If civil government be established here and military rule withdrawn, there is the greatest danger that the negro would become subject to some form of serfdom."

Mr. Commissioner McKaye, in his invaluable pamphlet, to which I have already referred, confirms the general correctness of the views of Colonel Hanks, and says they were concurred in by many other intelligent persons familiar with the subject, and that his own personal observation fully confirms them. He says:

"In a stretch of three hundred miles up and down the Mississippi, but one creole planter was found (there may, of course, have been others with whom I did not come in contact) who heartily and unreservedly adopted the idea of free labor, and honestly carried it out upon his plantation. And although he declared that, in itself, it was successful much beyond his expectation, yet, he said, 'my life and that of my family are rendered very unhappy by the opposition and contumely of my neighbors.'

"The simple truth is, that the virus of slavery, the lust of ownership, in the hearts of these old masters, is as virulent and active to-day as it ever was. Many of them admit that the old form of slavery is for the present broken up. They do not hesitate even to express the opinion that the experiment of secession is a failure; but they scoff at the idea of freedom for the negro, and repeat the old argument of his incapacity to take care of himself, or to entertain any higher motive for exertion than that of the whip. They await with impatience the withdrawal of the military authorities, and the reëstablishment of the civil power of the State, to be controlled and used as hitherto for the maintenance of what to them doubtless appears the paramount object of all civil authority, of the State itself, some form of the slave system.

"With slight modification, the language used recently by Judge Humphrey in a speech delivered at a Union meeting at Huntsville, Alabama, seems most aptly to express the hopes and purposes of a large proportion of the old masters in the valley of the Mississippi who have consented to qualify their loyalty to the Union by taking the oath prescribed by the President's proclamation of amnesty. After advising that Alabama *should at once return to the Union by simply rescinding the ordinance of secession,* and after expressing the opinion that the old institution of slavery was gone, Judge Humphrey says, 'I believe, in case of a return to the Union, we would receive *political coöperation,* so as to secure the management of that labor by those who were slaves. *There is really no difference, in my opinion, whether we hold them as absolute slaves or obtain their labor by some other method.* Of course we prefer the old method. But that question is not now before us.'"

To the same effect was the testimony of the late Brigadier General James S. Wadsworth, whose official tour through the valley of the Mississippi gave him ample means of arriving at an intelligent judgment:

"There is one thing that must be taken into account, and that is, that there will exist a very strong disposition among the masters to control these people and keep them as a subordinate and subjected class. Undoubtedly they intend to do that. I think the tendency to establish a system of serfdom is the great danger to be guarded against. I talked with a planter in the La Fourche district, near Tibadouville; he said he was not in favor of secession; he avowed his hope and expectation that slavery would be restored there in some form. I said, 'If we went away and left these people now do you suppose you could reduce them again to slavery?' He laughed to scorn the idea that they could not. 'What' said I, 'these men who have had arms in their hands?' 'Yes,' he said; 'we should take the arms away from them, of course.'"

While we confront these facts, let me, Mr. Speaker, ask of you and the House whether we shall best consult our country's welfare by giving to the laboring people of the South the ballot by which they may protect themselves, and inspiring them with the hopes and disciplining them by the duties of citizenship, or by predetermining that ours shall be a military Government, and that the first-born son of every northern household shall be liable to pass his life in the Army, maintained to protect the aristocratic South against the maddened and degraded laborers whom she oppresses. It is we who are to decide this question; we who are to determine who shall select delegates to the conventions that are to frame the future constitutions of the insurgent States; we who are to say whether the constitutions which they will submit to us when asking readmission are republican in form, as required by the terms of the Constitution of the United States; and if we fail here, to our timidity, arrogance, prejudice, or pride of color will be justly attributable the conversion of our peaceful country into a military Power, and our democracy into an aristocracy. "We cannot escape history."

This is not mere idle fancy. Let us for a moment suppose, not what is alone within the range of possibility, but what is within the scope of probability; nay, what is almost certain to happen—that the two hundred and ninety-one thousand pardoned rebels of South Carolina should demand from their Legislature an act reducing to apprenticeship, serfdom, or other form of slavery, the four hundred and twelve thousand colored people of the State, or that they deny them all political rights, tax them without their consent, legislate, not for their welfare, but for their degradation and oppression. Composing this unrepresented mass would be those who have passed through General Saxton's schools and learned to read, those who by toil have earned the means to purchase at sales for taxes, or under the confiscation laws, a home and land; and others scarred and warworn in the military or naval service of the country, who would hurry to and fro, rallying their friends to resist the outrage, and maintain their right to life, liberty, and property. Here would be the beginning of civil war; war in which we who believe in the doctrine of man's rights, that Governments are instituted to protect those rights, that they rest on the consent of the governed, and should be overthrown when they infringe those rights, would bid the insurgents God-speed. Ah! this we might do as men, as individuals; but as citizens of the United States what would be our duty and how must our power be exercised? The minority, though vested with political power, fearing the superior force of the majority, would, in the name of the State, appeal to us; and, repugnant as the duty might be, we would owe it to the sacred compromises of the Constitution to yield our pride, our conscience, our fidelity to God and man, and become again the protectors of slavery or the pliant instruments for reducing the majority of the people of the State into subjection to the arrogant aristocracy of South Carolina. In God's name let us, while we can, avert such a possibility. Let us conquer our prejudices. Let us prove that we are worthy of the heritage bequeathed us by our revolutionary sires. Let us show the world that, inheriting the spirit of our forefathers, we regard liberty as a right so universal and a blessing so grand that, while we are ready to surrender our all rather than yield it, we will guaranty it at whatever cost to the poorest child that breathes the air of our country.

But we owe a provision of this kind to another class of citizens than that of which I have been speaking. There are other loyal men than these in the South. Andrew Johnson, Horace Maynard, William H. Wisener, sr., John W. Bowen, W. G. Brownlow, though not alone in their loyalty, represent but a minority of the white people of Tennessee; and Thomas J. Durant, and Benjamin F. Flanders, and Rufus Waples, and Alfred Jervis have had thousands of adherents and coworkers among the whites of Louisiana; but they, too, are but a minority of the white people of that State. And as our armies go on conquering, we may learn that even on some hillside in South Carolina there have been men whose loyalty to the Union has never yielded. How shall these protect themselves in the reconstructed State? What millennial influence will induce the envenomed spirit of the majority of the people by whom they will be surrounded to treat them with loving-kindness or human justice? Who will go with them to the polls in their respective districts? Where will they find an unprejudiced judge and an impartial jury to vindicate their innocence when falsely accused or maintain their right to character and property? We must remember that it is the power and not the spirit of the rebellion we are conquering. Time alone shall conquer this. The grave, long years hence, will close over those who to the last day of their life would, were it in their power, overthrow the Government or revenge their supposed wrongs upon those who aided in sustaining it. The truly loyal white men of the insurrectionary districts need the sympathy and political support of all the loyal people among whom they dwell, and unless we give it to them we place them as abjectly at the feet of those who are now in arms against us as we do the negro whom their oppressors so despise. I cannot conceive how the American Congress could write a page of history that would so disgrace it in the eyes of all posterity as by consenting to close this war by surrendering to the unbridled lust and power of the conquered traitors of the South, those who, through blood, terror, and anguish, have been our friends, true to our principles and our welfare. To purchase peace by such heartless meanness and so gigantic a barter of principle would be unparalleled in baseness in the history of mankind.

This is felt in the South. The black man already rejoices in the fact that, if we are guilty of so great a crime as this, he will not be alone in his suffering; it will not be his prayers or his curses only that will penetrate the ear of an avenging God against those who had thus been false to all His teachings and every principle they professed. I find in the New Orleans Tribune of December 15, 1864, which paper, I may remark, is the organ of the proscribed race in Louisiana, and is owned and edited and printed daily in the French and English language by persons of that race, an admirable article in response to the question, "Is there any justice for the black?" which was drawn forth by the acquittal of one Michael Gleason, who had been tried for murder.

The crime was established beyond all peradventure. It was abundantly proven that the victim, Mittie Stephens, a colored boy, had been quietly sitting on the guards of the boat, watching the rod with which he was fishing, that other boys sat near him, when the defendant came behind him, leaned over, and deliberately pushed him into the water, and folding his arms on his breast stood and saw the boy rise thrice to the surface and then sink forever; that a colored woman exclaimed, "That is not right," and the defendant answered, "I would do the same to you;" and thus neither rescuing the child nor permitting others to do it, coolly and deliberately committed murder. There was no dispute as to any of the facts of the case. The New Orleans Era, noticing the case, says that it establishes the theory that "a man may, whenever he has no other way of amusing himself, throw a negro boy overboard from a steamboat, prevent any of his friends from rescuing the drowning struggler, stand quietly looking on while he goes to the bottom to rise no more, and be considered 'not guilty' of murder or any other crime;" and adds, having evidently hoped for better things under freedom than it had been used to in the days of slavery, "This is almost as enlightened a verdict as we were accustomed to in the palmy days of thuggery."

The colored editor of the Tribune avails himself of the case to point a moral, and well says:

"The trial by jury is considered as the safe-guard of innocence. It has been found that a man indicted for a criminal offense cannot be impartially tried and convicted, unless by his own peers. But an *ex parte* jury is the worst of all judicial institutions.

"The security afforded by the composition of a jury has to be of a twofold character. The jurymen have to represent the community at large in all its classes and varieties of composition. The duty of a jury is as well to vindicate innocence and punish crime as to protect the man unduly arraigned before the Court. Justice has to strike the culprit and avenge the blood of the innocent, as well as to defend the accused party against undue prejudices. Why have we no representatives in the jury? Are our lives, honor, and liberties to be left in the hands of men who are laboring under the most stubborn and narrow prejudice? Is there any protection or justice for us at their hands? It is in vain that, in the present instance, the press have so strongly supported the right. The wrong has been committed, and we are notified that there is no redress for us.

"*But for every Union man in the city the last verdict is a warning. In the event—as impossible as it may appear—that rebel rule should temporarily be established here, we can foresee the fate of the friends of the Union. Then, there will be no more justice, no more protection for them than for the hated negro. It will be lawful to pursue them in the streets, drown them, kill them; and no jury will be found to convict the murderers.* Let the Union men understand the case, and look to a complete reform in our laws relating to the formation of the jury."

The fate predicted to the real friends of the Union will be meted to them by the pardoned rebels, who will if we permit it rule them in the future as assuredly as it would if their military power should again possess the city.

Still comes the question, are these more than two fifths of the people of the insurrectionary district fit for citizenship? Let me reply by a question or two. Is the question of fitness put to the foreigner by the judge who administers the oath, the taking of which invests him with all the power of a native-born citizen and all its promises save one, that of the Presidency? Is the white native of our soil who, at the close of a reckless youth, the victim, perhaps, of early poverty and the degradation of parents, is unable to read his native tongue, when first he comes to the polls to deposit his ballot interrogated as to his fitness? Is it only to the wise, the learned, the powerful that we accord the right of suffrage? Are there not within the knowledge of each one of us scores of the children of this proscribed race who, in the conduct of their daily affairs, in the acquisition of property, in the tenderness and good judgment with which they rear their families, in the generosity with which they contribute to their church and the fidelity with which they obey her high behests, prove themselves infinitely better fitted for citizenship than the denizens of the swamp, Mackerelville, and other such reeking localities, who swelled the majority in the city of New York at the last election to thirty-seven thousand? And shall no culture, no patriotism, no wisdom, no tax-paying power, secure to the native-born American that which at the end of five years we, with so much advantage to our country, fling as a boon to every foreigner who may escape from the poverty and oppression and wrong of the Old World, to find a happier home and a more promising future in this? The question is not whether each man is fitted for the most judicious performance of the functions of citizenship, but whether the State is not safer when she binds all her children to her by protecting the rights of all and confiding her affairs to the arbitrament of their common judgment.

But colored people have shown themselves abundantly capable of self-government. Under oppressions exceeding in infinite degree those suffered by the oppressed people of Ireland—ay, by the subjects of the Czar of Russia—they have shown themselves capable of caring for themselves and others. Buying the poor privilege of providing for themselves by paying to their owners hundreds of dollars per annum, thousands of them have maintained homes and kept their families together, and reared their children to such an age that the lordly master, wanting cash for current purposes, has plucked the graceful daughter from her home to sell her to a life of debauchery, or the son, whose developing muscles promised support in age to his parents, to sell him to a life of unrequited toil. Snatched from these horrors a few thousands, some ten or twelve, have been sent during the last forty years to the western coast of Africa. There, under the auspices of American benevolence, they founded a republic, and with almost American greed for land have extended the jurisdiction of the little colony till the republic of Liberia, as I learn from the National Almanac, now embraces twenty-three thousand eight hundred and fifty-nine square miles. And the people have assimilated from among the heathens among whom they were settled men, women, and children, until their flag protects and their jurisdiction regulates four hundred and twenty-two thousand, most of whom, taught in the schools of the colony, find their enduring hopes in the old King James Bible, which they are able to read. But for our jealous contempt of the race, the flag of that African republic, so extensive has her commerce already become, would be familiar in all our leading ports. Our arrogance has hitherto excluded it; and by reason of our arrogance we pay tribute to our haughty commercial rival and treacherous friend Great Britain, by purchasing at second-hand from her the tropical products which the republicans of Liberia would gladly exchange directly with us for those of our more temperate region.

Fit by culture and experience they may not be; but let us regard the characteristics of our civilization and see whether the future should, by reason of this fact, be made liable to such momentous consequences as would be involved in error on this point. The abundant proof is before us of their eagerness and ability to acquire information. We are equally able to provide them with the means of culture; and happily, the good people of the North, carrying the frame of the school-house and the church in the rear of each of our advancing armies, have shown themselves prompt to provide them with the means of instruction—to give to each and every one of them the keys to all knowledge in the mastery of the English language, the art of writing, and the elementary rules of arithmetic.

Though the gentleman from New York [Mr. Brooks] insists that history is but repeating itself, I tell him that ours is a new age, and ask him to be kind enough to let me know who invented Hoe's "last fast printing-press" in the age in which it first existed, and by whose steam-engine it was propelled, and whether he edited the Express that fell in myriad thousands from its revolving forms? The limits of what former America did the magnetic telegraph traverse, making man, even the humblest, well-nigh omnipresent within its limits? In what antique age and country, broad as ours, was distance reduced as it is by the locomotive engine in this? From among the hidden treasures of what buried city, or from the printed pages of what lost nation, did John Ericsson steal the subtle thoughts with which he has blessed the world and which we credit to him as inventions? In what era, will the gentleman tell me, did a nation convert by the stroke of a pen and the act of occupancy its landless and destitute people into independent farmers and pillars of the State by a homestead law such as that by which we offer estates to the emigrant and the freedman? If history be but repeating herself, will the gentleman point me to the original of the American Missionary Society, and show me from experience what influence its labors are to have upon those whom we have hitherto doomed to the darkness of *ignorance*? Whence did the founders of the American and other Tract Societies borrow the idea of their great enterprise? From what age or what clime comes our common school system? And what chapter of human history did they reënact who founded the American Sunday School Union? Will the gentleman draw from his historic stores a sketch of the influence that institution alone is to have in developing and training the intellect and regulating the life of the freedmen and the "poor white trash," now that rebellion has opened the way to the teacher, the daily journal, and the printed volume to their firesides? In what ample depository did its ancient prototype conceal the stereotype plates for more than a thousand books that it so cheaply published, imparting many of them in the simplest sentences, and others in those of Bunyan, Milton, Heber, Cowper—the poets, preachers, philosophers, historians of all Christian countries—the thought and knowledge time has garnered?

No, Mr. Speaker, history is not repeating itself. We are unfolding a new page in national life. The past has gone forever. There is no abiding present; it flies while we name it; and, as it flies, it is our duty to provide for the thick-coming future; and with such agencies as I have thus rapidly alluded to, we need not fear that even the existing generation of freedmen will not prove themselves abundantly able to take care of themselves and maintain the power and dignity of the States of which we shall make them citizens.

We are to shape the future. We cannot escape the duty. And "conciliation, compromise, and concession" are not the methods we are to use. These, alas! have been abundantly tried, and their result has been agitation, strife, war, and desolation. No man has the right to compromise justice; it is immutable; and He whose law it is never fails to avenge its compromise or violation. Ours is not the work of construction, it is that of reconstruction; not that of creation, but of regeneration; and, as I have shown, the principle of the life we are to shape glares on us, lighting our pathway, from every page of history written by our revolutionary fathers. Would we see the issue of "compromise, concession, and conciliation?" Sir, we behold it in the blazing home, the charred roof-tree, the desolate hearthside, the surging tide of fratricidal war, and the green mounds beneath which sleep half a million of the bravest and best loved of our men.

South Carolina, representing slavery, demanded the insertion of the word "white" in the fundamental articles of our Government. Our fathers resisted the demand; and, as I have suggested, had their sons continued to do so, slavery had long since been hemmed in as by a wall of fire; its true character would have been known among men, for then would the freedom of discussion not have been assailed, and men been legally punished by fine and imprisonment, and lawlessly by scourging and death, for speaking of its horrors. And by resisting this demand, as I have shown, man was accorded his right in the Territories till 1812. Then our fathers yielded, and without tracing the rapid retrograde career which ensued, we find the results of conceding and compromising principle in the attempt to abandon justice as established by the fathers, and settle a Territory under the conflicting theories of Cass and Douglas, and of Calhoun and Jefferson Davis—the two former striving to establish slavery under phrases full of professed devotion to freedom; the latter proclaiming boldly, through the lips of Robert Toombs, that "Congress has no power to limit, restrain, or in any manner to impair slavery; but, on the contrary, it is bound to protect and maintain it in the States where it exists and wherever its flag floats and its jurisdiction is paramount." (Boston Address, January, 1856.)

We can trace the influence of compromise and concession again in its effects upon the constitution of States. Behold the colored and white voters mingling peaceably at the polls in North Carolina, Maryland, Tennessee, and other slave States, and run the downward career until, at the dictation of South Carolina and slavery, you find States which have become free by constitutional amendment and others which never tolerated slavery yielding to their demand to insert the word "white" in their constitutions, and so creating a proscribed class in their midst; others even denying a dwelling place upon His footstool within their limits to the children of God whose skins were not colored like their own; and finally Arkansas writing a chapter of history which redeems Draco's name from the bad preëminence it had so long borne. Triumphant wrong is ever aggressive, has ever been, will ever be. Look back also upon our churches, practically ignoring for half a century the existence of nearly four million people who were held in contempt of every one of the beatitudes, and compelled to live in violation of every clause of the decalogue, and whose existence made the utterance of the Lord's prayer seem, to foreigners who comprehended the wrongs of slavery, like a hideous mockery as it dropped from American lips.

And these results, be it remembered, did but express the influence which aristocratic and dictatorial South Carolina, whose spirit now possessed the entire South, had, through compromise, concession, and conciliation, produced upon the mind and heart and conscience of the American people. Let me illustrate this by one striking example. While yet Missouri was a Territory—seven years, however, after the South had been made imperious by her triumph in inserting the word "white" in the territorial law for Missouri, and while she was busy fashioning that great State north of the Ohio line into the future home for slavery—the abolition of the institution was being agitated in Maryland as well as in Tennessee. Notwithstanding the recent triumphs of slavery it was still possible for a man to oppose the spread of the institution, point out its atrocities, and favor its abolition, and yet look for preferment and honor at the hands of his fellow-citizens; and when Jacob Gruber, a Methodist clergyman, was indicted by the Frederick county court, of Maryland, on the charge of "attempting to excite insubordination and insurrection among slaves," Roger B. Taney stepped forth to defend him, and in the course of his argument used the following language:

"Mr. Gruber did quote the language of our great act of national independence, and insisted on the principles contained in that venerated instrument. He did rebuke those masters who, in the exercise of power, are deaf to the calls of humanity; and he warned them of the evils they might bring themselves. He did speak with abhorrence of those reptiles who live by trading in human flesh, and enrich themselves by tearing the husband from the wife, the infant from the bosom of the mother; and this I am instructed was the head and front of his offending. Shall I content myself with saying he had a right to say this? that there is no law to punish him? So far is he from being the object of punishment in any form of proceedings, that *we are prepared to maintain the same principles, and to use, if necessary, the same language here in the temple of justice*, and in the presence of those who are the ministers of the law. A hard necessity, indeed, compels us to endure the evils of slavery *for a time*. It was imposed upon us by another nation while we were yet in a state of colonial vassalage. It cannot be easily or suddenly removed. Yet while it continues, *it is a blot on our national character*, and every real lover of freedom confidently hopes that it will be effectually, though it must be gradually, wiped away, and earnestly looks for the means by which this necessary object may be attained. And until it shall be accomplished, until the time shall come when we can point without a blush to the language held in the Declaration of Independence, every friend of humanity will seek to lighten the galling chain of slavery, and better to the utmost of his power the wretched condition of the slave. Such was Mr. Gruber's object in that part of his sermon of which I am now speaking. Those who have complained of him and reproached him will not find it easy to answer him, unless complaints, reproaches, and persecution shall be considered an answer."

But under the influence of the doctrine of "conciliation, concession, and compromise," the author of this language soon learned that for an ambitious man these brave and good words were folly and madness. Pure in his personal life, beautiful in the relations that characterized his family and his social circle, his history will never be forgotten; his name will ever head the list of "ermined knaves." Thirty-eight years after the Gruber case, in the chief temple of justice of our country, in the presence of her ministers, of whom he was himself the chief, when speaking of the free colored men of New England and those of their race throughout the country, he declared, in violation of all truth, that—

"The legislation and histories of the times, and the language used in the Declaration of Independence, show that neither the class of persons who had been imported as slaves nor their descendants, whether they had become free or not, were then acknowledged as a part of the people, nor intended to be included in the general words used in that memorable instrument.

"It is difficult at this day to realize the state of public opinion in relation to that unfortunate race which prevailed in the civilized and enlightened portions of the world at the time of the Declaration of Independence, and when the Constitution of the United States was framed and adopted. But the public history of every European nation displays it in a manner too plain to be mistaken.

"They had for more than a century before been regarded as beings of an inferior order, and altogether unfit to associate with the white race, either in social or political relations; and so far inferior, *that they had no rights which the white man was bound to respect.*"

Mr. Speaker, shall we in providing for the reconstruction of the Union, accept and proclaim as our faith the hideous dogma that four millions of our people have "no rights which the white man is bound to respect," or, in the very hour in which our arms are breaking the power of the rebellion, make any concession to the spirit that evoked it? South Carolina may shake her gory locks and bloody hands at us in impotent rage; but let us not quail before her now as we have done for the last half century. Through the lips of northern "Sons of Liberty" and members of the order of "American Knights," she demands that, as a graceful concession, we shall comply to-day with the proposition our forefathers rejected on the 25th of June, 1778, and insert the word "white" in the fundamental law of the land; on the other hand, the shades of our patriot fathers, humanity, the spirit of the age, the welfare of the nation, the hopes of the countless millions who will throng our country through the long ages, implore us to listen to the voice of justice and obey the injunctions of the Master, who has assured us that "inasmuch as ye have done it unto one of the least of these my brethren, ye have done it unto me." Let not, I pray you, the South achieve her grandest triumph in the hour of her humiliation. Let not the spirit of a prostrate foe practice on our pride and prejudice, and exult through all time over a lasting victory. Peace is the offspring and handmaid of Justice, and let us in reconstructing the Union erect a temple in which she may abide for ever.

Mr. STILES. Mr. Speaker, I did not desire to interrupt my colleague [Mr. KELLEY] in the delivery of his carefully prepared speech. It would have marred its beauty and power. But if I understand him correctly he stated that prior to the adoption of the constitution of 1838, negroes enjoyed the right of suffrage in the State of Pennsylvania. My question is, whether the constitution or laws of that State gave them such a right; and further, whether they ever did exercise such a right; whether he does not know that by the decision of the highest courts of that State they were not allowed to vote there.

Mr. KELLEY. They were allowed by the constitution to vote, and they did vote; and it required a constitutional amendment—the insertion of the word "white" in the clause regulating suffrage—to deprive them of that right.

Mr. STILES. I desire to ask my colleague further, when and in what portion of the State of Pennsylvania they ever exercised that right.

Mr. KELLEY. Why, I have seen them exercise it frequently at the polls in Philadelphia, and that, too, whether the election officers belonged to one party or the other.

Mr. STILES. That must have been confined to my colleague's own precinct. It was never known in the history of that State.

Mr. KELLEY. I beg leave to say that it was done throughout the State, and was in some instances made the subject of litigation.

Mr. STILES. It was never done except in one county—the county of Bucks—so far as I know and then only in one instance.

I desire further to ask my colleague in this connection, because his speech has tended toward universal equality, whether he is in favor of giving negroes universally the right of suffrage now.

Mr. KELLEY. I am in favor of giving that right, in the words of Jefferson, to "every man who fights or pays." I stand by the doctrine of Thomas Jefferson, the father of the Democratic party, in which I was trained.

Mr. STILES. In the event of the passage of the amendment to the Constitution proposed, is my colleague in favor of equality between the races? And will he regard negroes as equal to the white man?

Mr. KELLEY. I could not possibly regulate the equality of men. I cannot make my colleague so moral or intelligent as a man of darker complexion who is more moral and more intelligent; nor could I degrade my colleague to the level, in morals and intelligence, of the colored man who is less moral or less intelligent than he. My colleague does not, according to his theory, vote by reason of his intelligence, but simply by reason of his color. I might be willing to exclude from the privilege of voting an immoral or a voluntarily ignorant man; but I want no senseless rule that allows a fool or a scoundrel to vote if he be white, and excludes a wise and an honest man if he be black.

Mr. STILES. Mr. Speaker, the remarkable speech just delivered appeals to passion and not to judgment, and is in favor of a principle that in years hence will be regarded as the height of the fanaticism of these days. The right of negroes to become voters, jurors, and in all respects equal with the white man, is the favorite theory of the times and of the party in power. The day will come when the men who avow such principles will be condemned by the popular voice everywhere.

www.ingramcontent.com/pod-product-compliance
Lightning Source LLC
LaVergne TN
LVHW011147110826
845150LV00008B/2559

* 9 7 8 1 4 1 8 1 9 2 1 3 6 *